ARIEL—THE POSTWAR MODELS

NITON PUBLISHING

ARIEL— THE POSTWAR MODELS

Square 4, light and heavyweight singles and twins

Roy Bacon

Published by Niton Publishing
P.O. Box 3, Ventnor, Isle of Wight, PO38 2AS

First published in 1983 in Great Britain by Osprey Publishing Limited,
27A Floral Street, London WC2E 9DP
Member company of the George Philip Group

A CIP catalogue record for this book is available
from the British Library

ISBN 1 85579 010 6

Original edition :-
Editor Tim Parker
Design Roger Daniels
Reprinted by Crossprint Ltd., Newport, Isle of Wight

Contents

170
COV 132

Foreword by Sammy Miller

Alphabetically the Ariel is first in the British motor cycle enthusiasts dictionary, and for me it holds many happy memories, and I am very proud to have been associated with the Ariel company at Selly Oak and later Smallheath.

My association with Ariel's started in 1956 when I rode GOV 132 in the Scottish Six Days Trial. Preparing for the trial my James trials machine needed some gearbox parts, but the James spares department could not supply these so my road racing manager, Terry Hill, telephoned his old riding companion, Ernie Smith, at Ariel's and it was agreed that I should borrow an Ariel for the event. In those days it was trials riding in the winter and road racing in the summer, and after the works team pulled out of road racing in 1958 I took up a works contract of employment with Ariel Motor Cycles, Selly Oak, and working in the competition workshop was every young man's dream come true.

I still remember vividly my first trip to Selly Oak which started off in Belfast on the night boat to Liverpool. I made an early start in the morning, riding GOV 132, with a rucksack on my back and heading south towards the Big Smoke. It was a bit of a daunting trip, and I could not believe the vastness of Wolverhampton and Birmingham.

I spent most of my first two months surrounded by turnings and filings, as the great lump of a trials horse was turned into a racing thoroughbred.

The incomparable Sammy Miller concentrating on the line ahead regardless of the rain in the Scottish Six Days. He rides the famous Ariel GOV 132

The late Ken Whistance was always a father figure to me and looked after me like a son, and Ernie Smith the competition manager even put me up in his home until I found digs in Hall Green.

It was a very happy unit, with Clive Bennet assisting Ernie Smith, and later, on Ernie's promotion to sales, Clive was in charge of the competition department and later the development shop, into which I moved when the competition department was closed, working on the development of many projects, with tongue in cheek wondering where the designers got their ideas from on such projects as the Pixie, Beagle, 350 Twin and the Flat 4.

One little project I did myself behind closed doors was an Ariel Arrow engine in a duplex frame, with BSA QD wheels and forks. I made it a semi-trail bike with upswept exhaust pipes and alloy tank, using this for my daily transport between Hall Green and Selly Oak. This machine created considerable interest and all the dealers who saw the machine were really enthusiastic, much to the embarrassment of the drawing department. This was in 1959, a 250 twin trail bike, probably 5 years in front of the Japanese, but after returning from the Scottish Six Days Trial that year I asked what had happened to my pet machine, only to be told it had been sawn up and thrown on the scrap heap, which proved that if ideas did not come from the drawing department they were flattened with a very heavy hand.

It was a sad day when Ken Whistance announced we had to close the Selly Oak factory and move to Small Heath to join the BSA workforce under one roof and streamline production of both the BSA and Ariel range. This move decimated the pride of the Ariel workforce, who were all quite anti-BSA.

For myself it provided me with more facilities than I had had at Selly Oak, and the recreation ground provided a marvellous practise area during my lunch break. Every day was spent practising sections and improving GOV 132, and also airing the BSA works 250 scrambler which Brian Martin kindly provided for me. This excellent little bike gave me many scrambles wins in the Midlands Centre, which was more than keenly contested with works BSA, James and Triumph riders all in the Centre.

Also it was very interesting to have Jeff Smith and Chris Vincent in adjacent workshops, as Chris was sidecar champion, Jeff was motocross champion and I was trials champion.

As the end approached I left to join Bultaco in 1964 and left behind many happy memories, and enjoyed my association with all the Ariel people. We had worked on many classic and interesting bikes. If only they were in business today with their marvellous fours and big singles!

I would not have changed those years for anything.

Sammy Miller
The world's most famous trials rider
New Milton, Hampshire
June 1983

Acknowledgements

In my youth I belonged to the local club and the chairman had a Red Hunter outfit that went everywhere with two-throttle positions—fully open and shut when the brakes were crammed on. The way that pre-war single withstood its treatment always stuck in my mind as the epitome of the tough Ariel.

Later on I rebuilt a Leader that had been stolen and dumped in a river and then changed this for an Arrow for production racing. This rattled its big ends out rather too quickly for a completely standard engine but the basics of a modern machine were always there and with development it could have continued. Unfortunately what it got was the heavy hand of the BSA empire and a sad ending.

A happier memory is of the immaculate Square Four used by the marshall at Aberdare race meetings of the fifties to conduct riders from the paddock to the start—and to fetch a plug if need be. Truly a machine to remember as representing the best of the marque.

Writing this book was made easy for me by Jim Lee the Ariel marque specialist. Not only did he check all the words, he also went through the appendices, provided some of the most interesting pictures and answered my telephone queries. My deepest thanks and gratitude go to him for he made my job possible.

The National Motor Museum at Beaulieu was once more a most useful reference and again I must thank the library staff for all their help with both information and pictures. Other picture sources were the Imperial War Museum, the Science Museum, London (two photographs of which are British Crown Copyright), Institute of Motorcycling and S. R. Keig in the Isle of Man but the bulk of them came as always from the magazines.

So I must thank Bob Berry and Peter Law of *Motor Cycle News*, Mick Woollett and Graham Sanderson of *Motor Cycle Weekly*, Mike Nicks of *Classic Bike* and Jim Lindsay of *Mechanics* for all their help. Among the pictures used were some taken by the professionals who were Cecil Bailey, Bermuda News Bureau, Ray Biddle, Steve Boom, Boswell Barratt and Phillips, Central Office of Information, Peter Hartley, J. L. Hewitt, Brian Holder, Edwin Lewzey & Co. and Donald Page.

As usual all the pictures were returned to their files after publication and I have tried to make contact to clear copyright. If my letter failed to reach you or I have used an unmarked print without knowing this, I can only apologise.

Finally I must thank Sammy Miller for kindly writing the foreword and for lending me some photos from his personal file. And again Tim Parker for organising me and the book into print.

Roy Bacon
Niton, Isle of Wight
June 1983

1 Siring the line

The Ariel slogan was 'The Modern Motorcycle' and after they adopted the prancing horse symbol they came from a stable that led the industry for a period in time. Their designs were versatile, sometimes unique, but also constant and left alone where this suited best. They built some very, very tough motorcycles in their time and deserved a better fate than to be 'nobbled' and then put down by company politics. A brief final reappearance of the name still brings a shudder to all those who rode the real machines from Selly Oak.

The company was one of the oldest of the English industry and like many had its roots in the cycle trade and city of Birmingham. The name Ariel was used as early as 1847 for a wheel, and again in 1871 for a pennyfarthing bicycle built in Coventry. It appeared on and off on bicycles for the next 25 years or more being used by a number of companies before the Ariel Cycle Company was formed in 1897. The company was owned by Dunlop Tyres and the new name was a sop to the rest of the cycle industry who objected to Dunlop Cycles while they virtually had to use Dunlop tyres and give their opposition free publicity. The machines themselves were made in Birmingham.

The Victorian nineties were a decade of great expansion in the cycle industry with frequent amalgamations and sales of company offshoots. One result was a manufacturing firm called Cycle Components which was located in Selly Oak and

The Ariel bicycles built by James Starley from 1871. Spokes are tensioned by hub cross-bar and machines held up by wires for this early photograph *(Science Museum, London)*

made parts in very large numbers. In 1895 they appointed Charles Sangster to their board and his family was to become one of the most important in the motorcycle industry.

In 1897 or 1898 Cycle Components bought the Ariel firm and in the latter year used the name for a powered tricycle they had constructed. As with many cycle firms, interest in the new forms of transport was sparked off by the Highways Act of 1896 which removed some of the obstacles, and Sangster and fellow director S. F. Edge were keen to be involved.

The first machine followed continental practice with single front wheel and, like many, fitted an engine built under licence from De Dion. However, unlike most, the Ariel had its engine located ahead of the rear axle so was more stable than the French original.

One machine was followed by a second and in 1900 by a quadricycle. This was essentially a tricycle fitted with twin front wheels and a passenger seat between them. The next year brought a genuine motor car, while the trike and quad continued and were joined by the first Ariel motorcycle. This used a Minerva engine with belt drive to the rear wheel and was fitted with pedals to assist it up the hills and when starting.

In 1902 the parent company changed its name to Components Ltd with Charles Sangster as managing director, and had two Ariel companies under its control, one concerned with bicycles and the other with the powered machines.

As the Edwardian decade progressed the Ariel Cycle Company took over the motorcycle business and phased out the trikes and quads, while the Ariel Motor Company concentrated on cars. In the middle of the decade they struck a bad patch as they over-produced in 1904 and money was tight the following year. To help sales Sangster encouraged the use of the Ariel in competitions and the firm had success in the Auto Cycle Cup race held in the Isle of Man in 1905. This was the first road race held there or on the mainland and after some 4 hours and 125 miles J. S. Campbell, riding a special Ariel with a vee twin JAP engine, won from Harry Collier by 16 seconds.

At the end of the era the Ariel range was replaced by one using White & Poppe engines with side valves in the T-head configuration. In 1911 Components bought the rights to the design and built the engines themselves and the range powered by these was joined in 1913 by a model with a vee twin engine suitable for sidecar use. This engine was changed to an Abingdon for 1914 and the model sold for solo use as well.

The firm continued to participate in sporting events with some success and their first continental award was won by John Young Sangster, the second son of the managing director. He was better known as 'Jack' and was to become one of the leading figures in the motorcycle industry, but was then studying motor engineering in France following an apprenticeship served at Selly Oak.

Like all manufacturing firms, Ariel were required to concentrate on war production once the conflict broke out but continued to build civilian motorcycles up to 1916. Car production ceased that year to make way for munitions, but many two-wheelers were supplied to the Army during the four years of war.

Early in 1919 Ariel began home deliveries once more, albeit of what was basically a prewar single, so were one of the first to be snapped up by transport hungry demobilized servicemen keen to spend their gratuity. For many the war had been their first real experience of transport and the mobility it could give, and having once had a taste they wanted their own machine.

By the end of the year Ariel had four models in their range, a single and a vee twin offered in solo or sidecar forms. They continued to enter competitions with some success but as the years progressed their machines did not. There were changes in models, capacity and details but the essence of the single in particular with its wide set valves and T–head remained unaltered.

Jack Sangster rejoined the firm late in 1922 following his army service and a period with Rovers, and became involved with the reappearance of the Ariel car. The first model, the Ariel Nine, had a flat twin engine and was followed by the Ten with a more conventional in-line four. These were built up to 1925 but the competition from the mass-produced Austin and Morris reduced sales to a trickle so production stopped.

With the end of the cars and a motorcycle range that had stagnated and still had a veteran air, the company fortunes were at a low ebb and they could easily have failed. So Charles Sangster acted and took on two men, Val Page and Vic Mole, who were to transform the company and push it right to the forefront of the industry.

Val Page was a quiet, modest gentleman and a brilliant designer and engineer who spent his working life with motorcycles following early days on the drawing board with Clement-Talbot cars. In 1908 he began riding on a home built machine and a little later went to the J. A. Prestwich firm at Tottenham where he worked on the JAP car which never went into production. During the war he did a spell with the Air Ministry and then returned to JAPs as chief designer.

He had to argue the case for big valves for better breathing with J.A.P. himself but persisted for at Clement-Talbot he had learnt that they were one of the real secrets. He had also learnt of the problems of rotary valves and the experience kept him clear of such troublesome de-

Above **The 1898 Ariel tricycle with de Dion engine tucked in ahead of the rear axle to improve the weight distribution** *(British Crown Copyright. Science Museum, London)*

Below **The 1900 Ariel quadricycle as found for the Science Museum but clearly showing its trike ancestry** *(British Crown Copyright. Science Museum, London)*

The Ariel style as built up to 1925 with wide set valves, small brakes but all chain drive

vices in later years and saved him and his firms much time and money.

The big valve point was proved with a side valve 250 cc single that ran at 8000 rpm, quite unheard of in 1920 and that engine was also over-square at 70 × 64·5 mm, again unusual. Vivian Prestwich set records at Brooklands using it and reached a speed of 63·6 mph over the kilometre. Page went on to design the 8·45 vee twin engine used by George Brough for the SS100 model, and its more sedate 8·30 brother with side valves. They were typical of the man, straightforward and fully thought out so were sturdy and without weaknesses or odd trouble spots.

Around that time he also designed a twin cam engine in 250 and 350 cc sizes and the larger one propelled a New Imperial ridden by Le Vack into a good lead in the TT for two years in succession before gearbox failure put him out. At Brooklands the engines broke many records but none of this helped the firm to prosper much so they decided to close their racing department which meant that Val Page wanted a new job.

He went to Ariel late in the summer of 1925 with a brief to design new machines to show at Olympia in the autumn. To do the selling Sangster took on Vic Mole as Sales Manager and both new men were given a free hand. Mole had a fertile and imaginative brain and this was coupled with the energy and flair for marketing, publicity and sales.

They had little enough time to get ready so Page concentrated on new engines and kept the changes to the cycle side to a minimum. The engines were two in number, one a side valve of 557 cc capacity and 86·4 × 95 mm dimensions and the second with overhead valves, dimensions of 81·5 × 95 mm and capacity of 496 cc. Both had roller big ends, aluminium pistons and mechanical oil pumps and were of straightforward layout. A three-speed Burman gearbox was used and all chain drive with two shock absorbers in the transmission.

The frame was still the diamond pattern with Druid front forks so that side of things was still in the veteran mould, which was continued by the front mounting of the magneto. The one area Page did attend to was braking which had been very poor, so he adopted seven inch internal expanding drum brakes in both wheels.

The new machines went on to display with the slogan 'Ariel, The Modern Motor Cycle', and with

Earlier Ariel with chain-cum-belt drive, rim brakes and forward magneto

a new trademark in the form of the Ariel horse. For the next 30 years or more much of their advertising would feature the stylized horse emblem, stable talk and scenes associated with the turf and its environment.

The machines were a good deal faster than the earlier ones and were halfway to establishing the singles line for the life of the firm. They continued to do well in competition and during 1926 the firm took on Harry Perrey as competitions manager and he soon found himself participating in various stunts dreamed up by Vic Mole to publicize the firm.

The first of these was a plot for Harry to drive a sidecar outfit with passenger up the Snowdon rail track to the summit. An Ariel car had been the first to do this on four wheels and Vic wanted an Ariel to be the first on three. Despite some early opposition from the ACU they were able to go ahead and the mountain was duly climbed on 30th September, 1926.

The machine used was from the 1927 range and after the rush in 1925 Val Page had more time to refine the new engines and do something about the cycle parts. The main engine change was to resite the magneto behind the cylinder and to drive it by enclosed chain from the end of the single camshaft. This sat in a circular chamber on the timing side and was gear driven from the crankshaft. Bell crank levers transmitted the lift to the valves via push rods or tappets and the oil pump was driven off the end of the camshaft. This simple and easy to make engine design remained unaltered in its essentials throughout its long life and is yet another tribute to Page's design skills.

On the cycle side there was a new cradle frame and a new Burman gearbox which sat on the cradle under it instead of hanging from a seat tube. The exhaust system was changed also for in 1926 it was an uninspired object with minute silencer mounted well forward with a long tailpipe. In its place went a pipe that ran back to the rear wheel with a stylish Brooklands silencer attached to it. One model, the Super Sports, had a cylinder head with twin ports and a system on each side, then a fashion point.

The best part of the 1927 Ariel was the tank, a combined petrol and oil storage one. It was a saddle tank, inspired it is said by the HRD, but unlike its predecessors it was made from steel pressings welded together, the first English make

The 1926 Page Ariel engine whose basic design remained unchanged for over 30 years

to use this method. It transformed the appearance and was in at the start of a trend. The looks plus a very keen price ensured the machine's success and sales rocketed.

This did not stop Vic Mole from seeking publicity, and in 1927 he turned his attention to the Maudes Trophy. This was a silver vase, originally known as the Pettyt Cup, held by the ACU to be awarded each year to the firm that achieved the most meritorious performance in a test of reliability, economy, easy servicing and comfort. It had been presented by George Pettyt of Maudes Motor Mart in Exeter in 1923 to promote these characteristics as opposed to speed and racing and was won by Norton that year and for the next three.

In 1927 Ariel decided to do something about this and, like Norton, embarked on a long distance endurance run with a side valve machine with sidecar. The mileage covered was 5011 miles and the test lasted for 251·5 hours during which time the engine ran continuously. Not without problems which included a disintegrating sparking plug which Harry Perrey wired together, bandaged and varnished while the engine ran on. They won the trophy from thirty other firms who staged tests that year.

For 1928 the Ariel frame was redesigned as they had suffered some down tube breakages. The new design had straight tubes, some of increased size, and still gave the low saddle position of the earlier one. The engines were much quieter thanks to valve enclosure and increases in load carrying areas, while the silencer gained a fishtail which added its own contribution. The firm continued to prosper and Harvey Sangster, Jack's brother, toured the Far East and while in Japan rode his Ariel up Mount Saya San. In Scotland Ben Nevis was climbed by a sidecar outfit and many competition successes were gained throughout Britain.

Ariel again entered for the Maudes Trophy and ran a prototype 1929 model of 250 cc and also a 500 cc, both with overhead valves. They ran for 10,003 miles over 22 days and followed this with an hour at Brooklands. The company was awarded the trophy for a second time.

The 250 was given the name Colt and built in side and overhead valve form, proving to be a useful addition. New to the whole range was the adoption of dry sump lubrication with a twin plunger pump bolted to the inner timing case and driven by the end of the camshaft.

1929 was also the year of the depression, the appearance at Ariel of Edward Turner, and another Vic Mole publicity stunt. Turner, who was to become another of the leading figures of the industry, had a motorcycle background, having run a shop in London where he designed and built a face cam single. This brought him to the notice of Charles Sangster and Turner sold him on his ideas for a four cylinder machine with the pistons in a square four layout. Thus Turner was offered a job at Ariel to develop the idea under Val Page with the help of Bert Hopwood, another industry heavyweight, who did the drawings.

The outcome was the Ariel Square 4, a unique design that was to run on for many years as their top of the range model. Meanwhile, back in 1929, Vic Mole suggested to Harry Perrey that he rode an Ariel across the English Channel, so a standard 500 was mounted on a pair of floats with a drive

Above **The 1927 Ariel with rear magneto, cradle frame, better forks, styled exhaust and silencer, with big brakes whose size was kept from then on**

Below **Harry Perrey and Ted Thacker crossing the English Channel in 1929**

to a propeller. With Harry driving and Ted Thacker on the pillion they pushed off from Dover, crossed to Calais, rested briefly and then returned to England. The floats were 18 ft long and 2 ft wide with a similar size gap between them, and twin rudders were connected to the front wheel, but the device sailed itself and the two men could stretch their legs by walking on the floats.

This exploit gained them plenty of publicity and was backed up by many minor events and occasions when an Ariel would be manoeuvred into the act, a photo taken and more promotion won. It seemed that it did not matter what you did, as long as you were a known name you would find yourself pictured with an Ariel and in the papers.

The next trend in fashion was sloping engines, triggered by the BSA model of that name and for 1931 Ariel covered their bets by adding a number of slopers to the range with vertical engines. The Colt achieved the slope with a tilted engine but the 500 cc model was a redesign with more slope than anyone else and a four valve head.

However, the sensation on the Ariel stand at the Olympia Show held late in 1930 was the Square Four, or Squariel as it was immediately christened. It did not completely steal the show for, despite the economic depression, there was a second four making its debut at that show, the Matchless Silver Hawk with narrow vee layout and, like the Ariel, an overhead camshaft. However, the Ariel scored on price and was to remain in production for much longer.

After the heady atmosphere of the show came the dawn and the hard work of selling machines in difficult times. Vic Mole left the company and so there were no more outrageous stunts, but

Part of the 1931 Ariel Maudes Trophy attempt was for seven schoolboys to start the new four, seven times each. On 48 attempts it went first kick, once it needed two prods.

Above **The 1931 single with sloping engine and well splayed down tubes that could accommodate the four**

Below **1932 twin port single with vertical cylinder and frame with single downtube**

a Square Four was privately entered for the 1931 TT fitted with a supercharger. It was a rush to get the machine to the start and it retired in the race.

1931 was the year of the Ariel 7 test undertaken for the Maudes Trophy and this involved seven different models each undergoing a test with a seven feature in its make-up. It took about a month to carry them all out for they meant visits to Brooklands and trials hills as well as runs on the road, but at the end they gained the award once more.

Trading conditions became even worse that year as the depression bit and this affected the Sangsters for Charles was involved with Swift Cars which failed. Due to this he and Jack decided to diversify a little using the name Fleet, from one of their bicycles, on a three-wheel delivery vehicle. This new model used the 557 cc side valve Ariel engine to drive its single rear wheel with the goods suspended between the two front ones.

For 1932 a new name was given to the most sporting of the overhead valve singles—the Red Hunter and it was one that became well known and respected.

During the year the company's position worsened and Components had to go into liquidation. This placed their assets on sale and by hard negotiation Jack Sangster was able to buy the essentials of Ariel and set it going again as Ariel Motors (JS) Ltd. It was a sad and desperate time for him as his father died soon after, but the motorcycle company survived.

It did this by slimming right down and one man who left was Val Page who went to Triumph

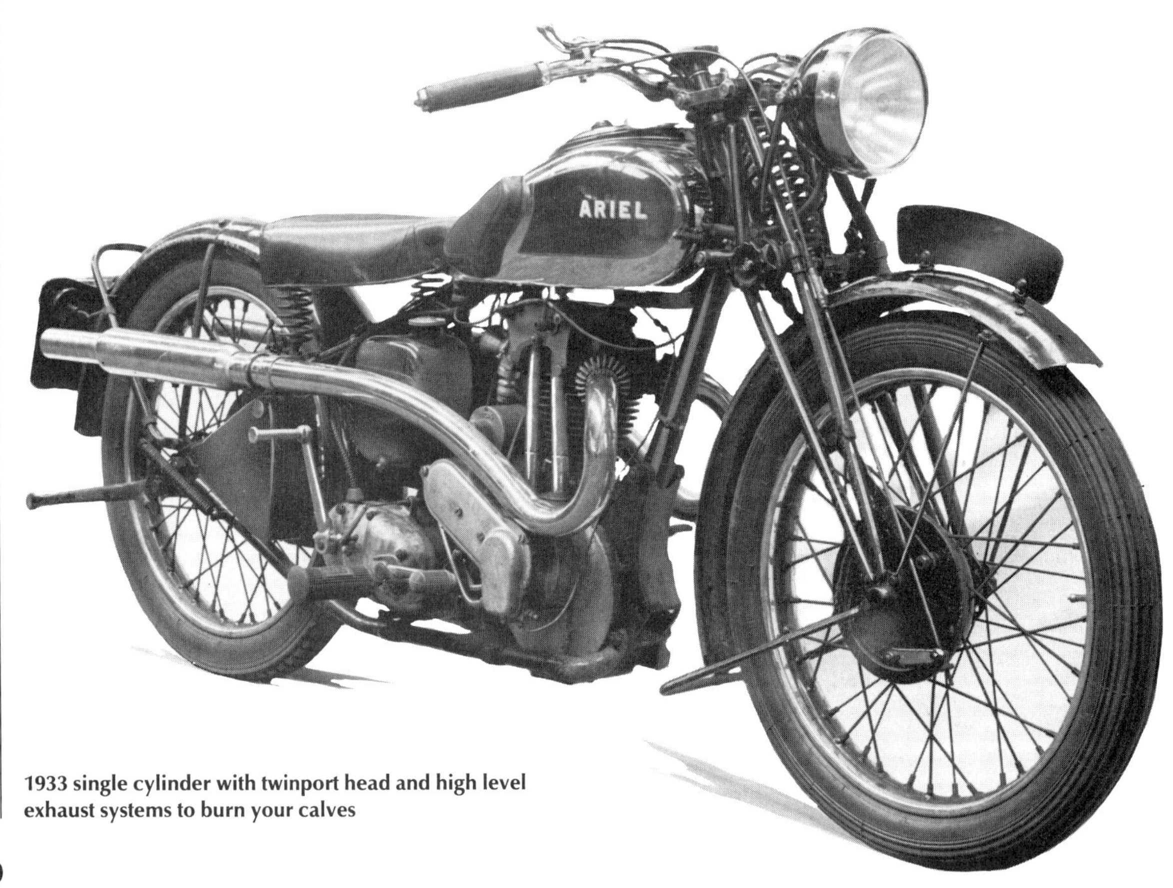

1933 single cylinder with twinport head and high level exhaust systems to burn your calves

Again 1933 and twin port, with typical armoured speedo drive rising from gearbox

where he designed a new range of singles and a 650 cc parallel twin that was the forerunner of its type. Edward Turner became chief designer at Ariel and then technical director, while Bert Hopwood was chief draughtsman.

For 1933 Ariel trimmed down their rather extensive range and it assumed the basic form that was to continue for the next quarter century. Thus they offered ohv singles in 250, 350 and 500 cc sizes in standard and sports Red Hunter finish. For the sidecar man there was a slightly larger side valve single and for the well-heeled the Square Four. Turner gave the Red Hunters upswept exhaust pipes and a sparkling finish to make them very attractive to the average clubman, and his flair for feeling the market worked as it was to many times again.

The new slimmer and fitter Ariel firm found that they had the right machines and so were able to run on through the thirties with few real changes. They continued to fare well in competition and at Brooklands gained publicity from the high speeds Laurence Hartley obtained from a side valve model, and the efforts of Bickell brothers to supercharge a Square Four and keep it from blowing its head gasket. It proved fast but never kept going for long enough to take the hour record they were after.

By 1935 the Ariel concern was in fine shape financially unlike Triumph who had overstretched themselves on the car side. They decided to stop motorcycle production but reckoned without Jack Sangster who decided to keep the name going. At the end of the negotiations Sangster owned Triumph Engineering, Edward Turner was installed in Coventry as its chief designer and general manager, and Bert Hopwood had joined him. Ariel had a new chief designer, Frank Anstey who had been with Triumph and previously with Rudge, while Val Page once more moved on. Page went to BSA where he designed the range of singles they were to build until unit construction came along and from that range came the famous Gold Star.

At Triumph Turner once again showed his talent for designing machines people bought, first by painting the singles silver and giving them the 'Tiger' label, and then with his immortal Speed Twin. The Tiger and the Red Hunter had much in common, with twin upswept exhaust systems and chrome plated supports at each side of the rocker box.

Above **The 1936 model VB with footchange and to change little in two decades**

Top **Left side of 1936 VB showing dry clutch and characteristic Ariel front number plate**

Right **VB engine, a full 600 for 1936, coupled to footchange gearbox but hand operation was available to special order**

At the end of 1936 the company took the name Ariel Motors which it was to keep for the rest of its days and continued with its range with little alteration, except for a redesign of the Square Four and the adoption of four-speed foot-change gearboxes for all models. 1938 brought a change in cylinder head and rocker box for the ohv singles but the essentials of 1926 were still clearly there.

1939 saw the introduction of rear wheel springing as an option for any machine in the range, except the 250 cc models. The suspension was by plunger springs linked to the rear spindle by links so that the rear chain tension remained constant and was designed by Anstey before he went to the Villiers firm that year. In his place returned Val Page from BSA and he worked on a pair of high camshaft singles being developed for the 1940 season.

Not for long, however, as the outbreak of war saw the Government garnering the firm's entire output and calling for a purpose-designed and built machine for despatch riders. So once again Val Page had to design against the clock and the result appeared in 1940, known as the model W/NG.

The machine was based on the standard 350 cc single amended to the form used in the ISDT with a competition frame and high ground

RAF Motor Transport working on W/NG Ariels in a French field next to the beaches. Note gentleman at ease on right with topee *(IWM)*

clearance. It was simplified by the deletion of some of the civilian features, given a pair of tool-boxes and fitted out with panniers and headlamp mask. With its trials frame it handled better off road than on and was much used by forward troops where it was best suited. Like all the War Department machines it was tough and many thousands of them went to war.

After the war many were sold off as war surplus but a smaller batch of 250 cc models failed to survive the conflict. Most machines of that size were used by the forces for training only.

During the war Val Page thought about post-war trends and came to two conclusions. One was that telescopic forks would be fitted to all machines and the other that Ariel would need a twin cylinder model in their range. So he laid out the basic design for the twin and designed the forks. There were built and tested during the war years and the same design went on to be used on Ariel, BSA and Sunbeam machines in postwar years.

The reason for this wide use was the sale of the Ariel firm to BSA late in 1944. The news caused a sit-down strike at Ariel until it was confirmed that the stable would stay at Selly Oak. Sangster remained a director of Ariel but the move gave him more freedom to concentrate on Triumph, while part of the deal was that he would give BSA first refusal on that concern should he ever wish to dispose of it. Eventually, in 1951, this was to happen and even later Jack Sangster was to become Chairman of the BSA group which controlled both Triumph and Ariel.

For Ariel this was all in the future and for many years they were to work in peace at Selly Oak before finally being drawn into the maelstrom of the BSA political whirlpool. Until then they got on with the job of building tough, hard working machines.

Instructor showing how not to ride under fire but what is possible even cross country *(IWM)*

2 Square 4

When Edward Turner decided to design a four cylinder motorcycle engine he chose a unique layout. His flair for what the buyer would put his money down for took him away from the width of a transverse engine with its ungainly chain line, or the length of the in-line motor with its cooling problem. A flat four meant shaft drive or costly bevels and a vee lacked the rigid construction of a crankcase joined to a one-piece cylinder block.

The square four offered the same good balance as the in-line plus very compact dimensions, while the four small even power impulses of the cylinders were far less destructive than the one thump of a single. Thus a small and light frame could be used along with light components throughout to keep the weight down and the performance up. This did leave the problem of coupling the crankshafts without gear rattle intruding as the crankcase warmed up and expanded, but in selling the idea of the four to Sangster, Turner also sold him the notion that a special gear tooth form would overcome this.

As originally schemed by Turner, the Square 4 engine was undoubtedly light and compact, being made even more so by the use of a three-speed gearbox built in unit with the engine. He coupled the two crankshafts together by cutting gear teeth on the central flywheel each had and the rear one drove the gearbox. So small and light was the assembly that it could, and did, fit into the 250 frame giving a very light motorcycle.

Unfortunately the unit construction layout was not an economic proposition and the cylinder head finning proved to be inadequate for sustained full throttle work.

So the production model first shown to the public at Olympia late in 1930 was more conventional as to its gearbox and heavier for it used the frame from the 500 cc sloper single. It still created a sensation for the engine had not only four cylinders but also an overhead camshaft, even if the rest of the machine was much more mundane with hand gearchange and the same fittings as the sloper. Fortunately the tilted engines had forced duplex down tubes to be used and their spacing was sufficient to span the crankcase of the four.

The engine of the four was based on dimensions of 51 × 61 mm giving a capacity of 498 cc and had overhung cranks for three of the cylinders. It had been so for all four on the prototype but for production the left rear crankshaft was given an outer web so it could drive back to the clutch and gearbox.

The two crankshafts were similar in concept with a large helical gear cut on the centre flywheel. This expensive gear cutting method was changed to spurs from engine 200 and in either case they were enclosed by an inner case and outboard of them sat a main bearing on each side. The main crankcase was split horizontally and the bearings clamped to the top half. Outboard of each bearing went a flywheel and this carried the crankpin with roller big end. The fourth crankpin was extended and joined its outer web in normal fashion, while the inner webs were secured to the central flywheels by nuts.

The 1931 Ariel Square Four. 500 cc, overhead camshaft, front carburettor feed by cross-tube and duplex frame tubes

The 600 cc Four of 1934, still with overhead camshaft and hand gearchange. Chain drives in alloy cases dominate right side

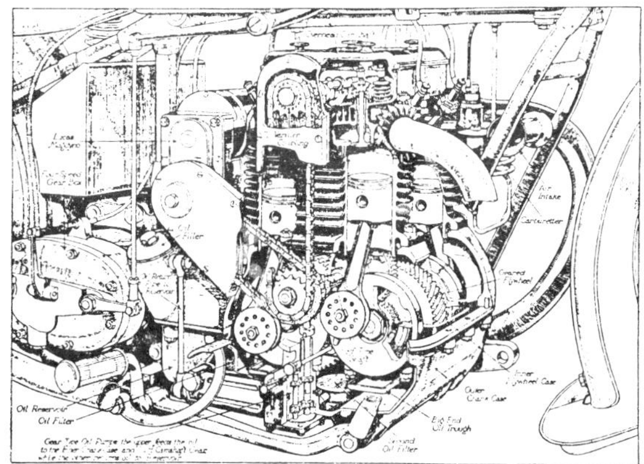

Line drawing of early Four showing geared crankshafts, half-time shaft and overhung big ends

The front crankshaft drove a half time shaft by gears and this was positioned between the cranks near the top of the case and ran from its centre out to the right. It carried a skew gear near its middle which drove to a gear oil pump set low down in the wet sump.

At the right end of the half time shaft went two sprockets, the inner driving the magneto situated behind the cylinder block and carrying a dynamo on its back, while the outer was connected to the camshaft. This ran in ball races in an aluminium cambox bolted to the cylinder head and carried eight rockers to move the vertical valves. The upper sprocket incorporated a vernier coupling and the cambox was closed by a top cover and lubricated by a separate feed from the oil pump. On the left end of the camshaft went a distributor for the ignition system and each drive chain was enclosed in a two-part aluminium case.

The cylinder head was cast in iron and separate from the one-piece block which was in the same material. The head carried the single Amal carburettor at the front between the two forward facing exhaust pipes, and the induction passage ran back to the centre of the casting where a cruciform porting system connected with the cylinders. The exhaust ports on each side connected together with an outer passage to feed into the pipe and Brooklands style silencer with fishtail that graced each side of the machine.

The lubrication system relied on the lower ends of the connecting rods dipping into oil

The 1937 1000 cc Four with all iron engine, pushrod valve operation and vertically split crankcase

troughs to feed the big ends which was quite a common practice at the time and removed the need to drill small holes through the crankshaft. The dippers were narrow section fingers that reached down from the steel rods and scooped the oil up and into drillways to the rollers. The oil itself was carried at the rear of the crankcase.

The complete machine featured a tank top instrument panel, common to the range, and a front number plate that was to characterise the marque for a long time. It did this by having a lower edge that followed the mudguard, top that was straight and not curved as usual but with a slight upwards tilt at the front end, vertical rear edge and curved front one that gave a flair and line that was instantly recognised anywhere.

For the rest the machine was as the 500 sloper with just a small re-arrangement to move the battery to the normal oil tank region to balance up the appearance. It made a successful debut and ran on into 1932 when it was joined by a larger version to satisfy a demand for more power for sidecar work. The newer model had a capacity of 601 cc and this was achieved by simply opening the bore up to 56 mm. Both it and the 500 had more finning than before and it was the 600 that was used in the Maudes test. The machine was set to cover 700 miles in as many minutes at Brooklands, and on the first try the engine seized before the halfway mark. A second unit was assembled with care that adequate clearance existed at all bearings, and this time all went well. After the test the machine covered a timed lap at 87·4 mph.

The slimmed down range of 1933 only had the larger four listed, although the 500 was said to be available to special order for a short while. Until they used up stocks of parts of course. The engine of the 600 had the straight teeth for the coupling gears and a change to a single plunger oil pump driven from the half time shaft. The oil was carried in the sump under the engine so the overall length came down and this allowed the standard 500 upright single cylinder frame to be used.

1934 brought rubber mounting of the handlebars for the four as well as the rest of the range and the model ran on to 1936 with only detail changes. It was intended to offer a new and larger four that year but development problems delayed it and Edward Turner, having designed it, had little time to spend on it with his move to Triumph and greater responsibilities. Thus it was delayed until 1937.

The new four was the model 4G, larger and completely redesigned. It had overhead valves, used dry sump lubrication and plain big ends. Only the basic layout stayed the same.

The new engine dimensions were 65 × 75 mm which gave a capacity of 995 cc. In place of the overhung big ends there were two forged crankshafts running in caged roller races on the left and white metal lined bronze bushes on the right, timing side. The two crankshafts were essentially the same and each had a central flange carrying a separate flywheel. This bolted to the right of the flange on the front crank and to the left on the rear which allowed the two flywheels to overlap and thus be of $6\frac{3}{8}$ in. diameter, although the cylinder centres were only 5 in. apart fore and aft.

To enable the flywheel to pass over the outer crankshaft web each had a separate balance weight which was dovetailed and bolted to it. The connecting rods were forged in RR56 aluminium alloy and had split big ends which were lined with white metal. The caps were retained by bolts with a ground diameter to act as the locating spigot and the nuts were locked with split pins. The small ends were bronze bushed and carried hollow, taper bored gudgeon pins which were retained in the pistons by circlips.

The pistons were in aluminium alloy and gave a compression ratio of 5·8:1 with two compression and one scraper ring on each. The long skirt was cutaway at the side to clear the flywheels. The pistons ran in a one-piece cast iron cylinder block with the centres at $4\frac{1}{2}$ in. across the frame, and eight studs held it to the crankcase. This was split vertically and cast in aluminium in conventional form despite the two cranks turning within it. The case joint faces were flat and dowels

600 cc overhead camshaft Four as in 1936. Much as the earlier version but with footchange

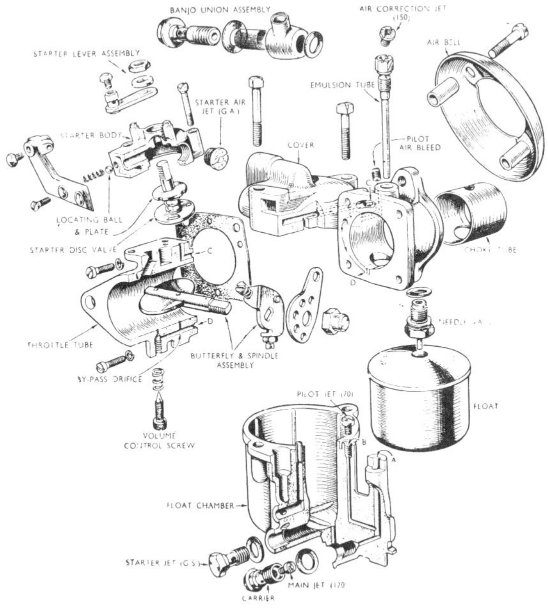

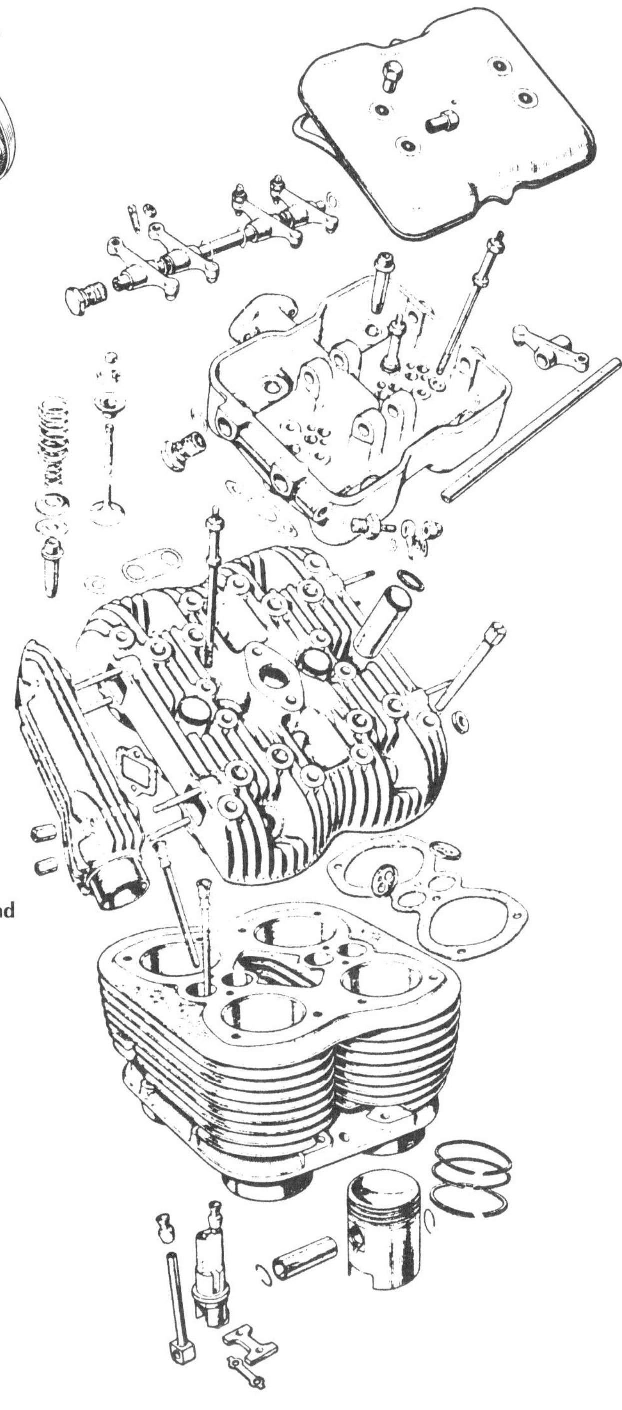

1000 cc Square Four details

Above **The Solex carburettor with multiple jets used for some years**

Right **The all iron top half showing the rocker box which the valve guides pin to the head. Tappet guides fit underside of block**

Far right above **The simple timing gear, oil pump drive and oil filter**

Far right below **Crankshaft coupling gears with discs to prevent gear ring, gear case door and connecting rod detail**

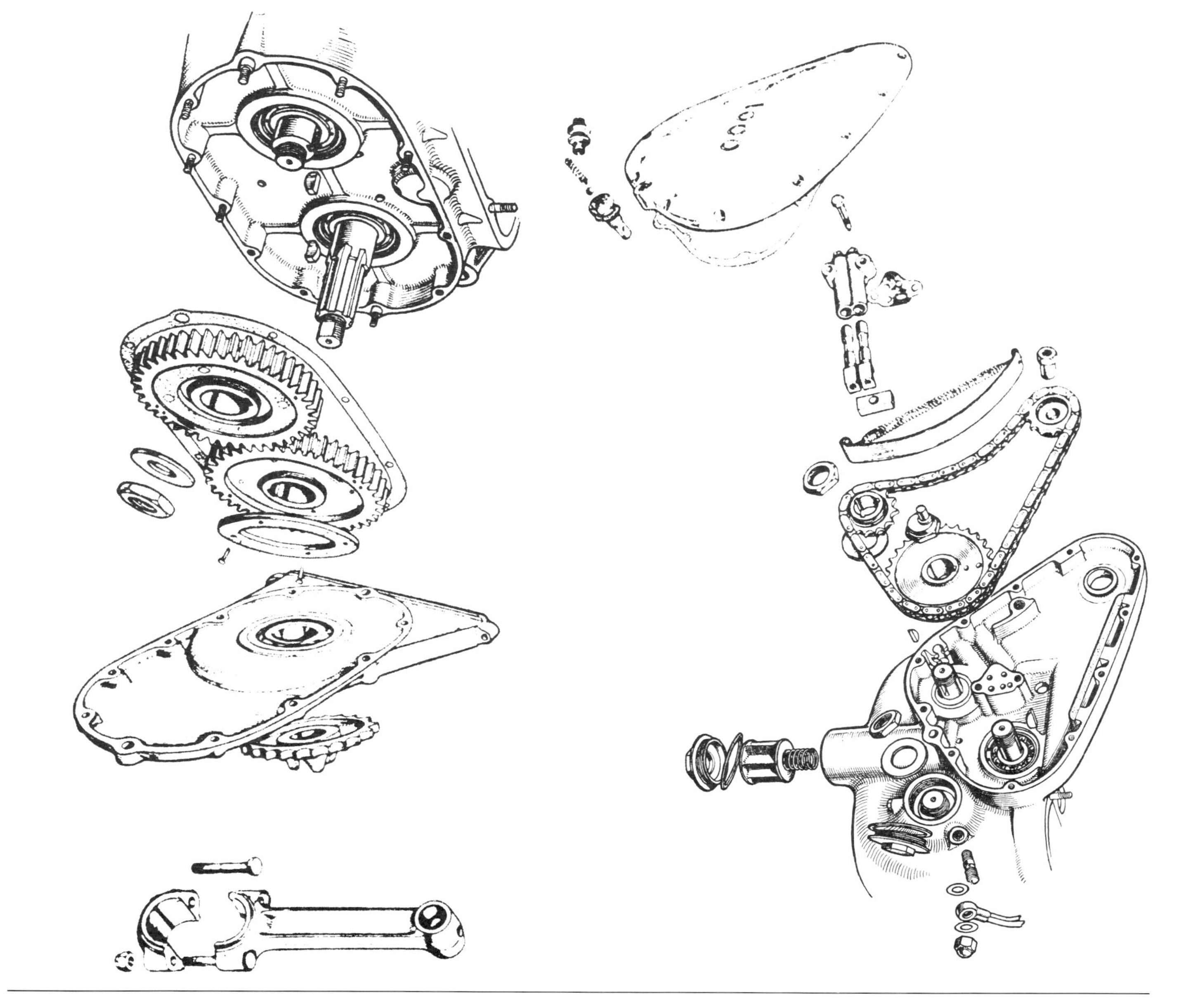

The 1939 Four in the rigid frame and girder forks also used in early postwar times

located the two halves together just as they aligned the cylinder block. As well as bolts all round the periphery of the crankcase, it was also joined by two fixings which bolted bridges between the cylinders together.

Below these ran the camshaft set across the engine in a ball race on the right and bush on the left. It was enlarged in the centre to reduce whip, but in truth needed a third and central bearing to reinforce the others. Above the camshaft sat four aluminium tappet blocks in a line, each pair held up in the cylinder block by a single bridge piece secured by two locked screws and carrying the tappets. These had square feet to prevent their rotation and the working face was radiused.

Cups sat on the top of the tappets and in them went the lower ends of the light alloy push rods. Further cups at the tops of these engaged with the rocker arms which had screw adjustors at their outer ends to bear on the hardened caps on the valve stems. All the valves were vertical and worked in guides pressed into the iron cylinder head.

The cylinder head was cast with the cooling fins running from front to back and the valves sat in two rows across it in pent roof combustion chambers with the sparking plugs angled fore and aft to aid access. The inlet tract was still of cruciform layout but the arms of the cross connected to a vertical passage cast into the top of the head. The four exhausts ran straight out to each side, which helped to reduce the heat feed back which had been a problem. They connected to a detachable cast manifold on each side and these were well finned and enhanced with chrome plated panels held by screws threaded into the long manifold nuts. Each manifold exited the gas at the front end into an exhaust pipe clamped to it by a finned collar and connected to a Brooklands-style silencer with fishtail end. Iron was the normal manifold material but aluminium was also tried for short while.

The rocker box was cast in aluminium and open topped. It was located to the cylinder head by the valve guides which passed through it into the head and each valve was restrained by twin coil springs retained by a collar and cottars. The rockers oscillated on two spindles set across the box and these were each supported by a pair of central bosses as well as at each end. The spindles were hollow and cross-drilled for lubrication with a supply banjo at the right end of each.

The first part of the induction tract was formed in the rocker box with a tunnel running from the rear into the centre of the box where it turned down to meet the cylinder head. The two parts were joined at this point by two bolts entered from below the head, while a further four long bolts secured both to the cylinder block. These bolts were extended up and located a lid onto the box to close it and this was secured by four sleeve nuts screwed to the bolts. External to the rocker box a further eight bolts held the head down onto two separate gaskets, one for each fore and aft cylinder pair, and between head and crankcase went four light steel tubes to enclose the push rods.

The inlet tract of the rocker box was flanged to carry the carburettor and this was not the usual Amal but a Solex which caused a good deal of confusion thanks to its butterfly throttle and many jets. It was still gravity fed and had a float chamber to control the fuel level.

The timing chest, on the right of the engine, was formed by extending the crankcase casting back to make a wall and attaching a cover to this with the number '1000' engraved into it. Inside the chest were three sprockets arranged in triangular form with a chain connecting them, one on the crankshaft, one twice as large on the camshaft, and a third on the mag-dyno. The chain was tensioned by a Weller flat spring itself bowed by a tension one and above the top run

Enlisted Squariel with headlamp mask and two-into-one exhaust pipe

went a fibre strip to prevent chain thrash.

The chest also contained the twin plunger oil pump which was driven by a pin machined eccentrically into the cap nut holding the camshaft sprocket in place. The system was changed to dry sump with an external oil tank, and the pump supplied the two plain main bearings from where a supply was taken via drillings in the crankshaft to the big ends. The pressure line contained a relief valve and after feeding the mains went on to an outlet where a banjo was connected with two pipes, one going to the rocker shafts via a single connection to the head and internal drillways, while the other went to a pressure gauge.

Oil drained from the rocker box to the sump via the push rod tubes, so lubricating the cams and tappets, and passed through a gauze filter in the sump before being pumped back to the tank. An engine breather pipe went into the back of the timing case but had little work to do as the under piston volume barely varied as the engine rotated.

The magneto was a twin spark type run at engine speed to fire the four plugs once in every two revolutions. It carried a dynamo on its back and incorporated in the drive to this was a distributor, skew gear driven and running at half engine speed. The electrics were 6-volt and dynamo control was by a regulator, then just introduced.

The two crankshafts were coupled by spur gears on the left running in their own compartment. Each gear had a fibre disc pressed into a recess in its side and held by rivets to prevent gear ring, and their compartment was closed by a door that also acted as part of the back of the primary chaincase. The door carried an outrigger roller bearing which supported the rear crankshaft that extended through it to the engine sprocket and its shock absorber. This race looked like a main but had a special bore smaller by one thou and this must have caused confusion over the years.

1947 Ariel advert for the Four showing it still with rigid frame and without pillion equipment

The primary transmission was by single strand chain to a dry clutch and a four-speed, footchange, Burman gearbox. The primary chaincase outer was an aluminium casting and had a separate dome for the clutch body which ran outside it. The body was attached to the chain wheel by a ring of six bolts and between the two sat the case wall. It was not quick to dismantle but did keep the clutch dry.

The gearbox was the Burman type BA and of conventional English form. Thus the clutch and final drive sprockets were both on the left and concentric, while the layshaft lay behind and below the mainshaft. Gear selection was by a pair of forks which sat on a barrel cam, each with a pin running in a guiding track. A gear at the end of the cam meshed with a quadrant which was moved by the positive stop mechanism.

The kickstarter mechanism comprised a gear with spring loaded face ratchet on the end of the mainshaft and this was turned by a quadrant on the pedal shaft.

The cycle parts continued on the lines of the heavier singles and the frame had a single down tube but duplex rails under the engine. It was still rigid with girder front forks and equipped with saddle, oil tank on the right, matching battery on the left and toolbox set between the chainstays on the right. Offset brake drums were fitted and an instrument panel was set in the top of the tank which was finished in red and chrome, this being matched by the wheel rims.

The result was a fast and smooth motorcycle. Top speed was a speedometer 100 with the occasional one reaching a genuine three figures, but most ran to the middle 90s. This was sufficient to see off nearly everything you were likely to encounter in a day's run, and do it in style. There was no need to scrabble for gears for from as little as 10 mph in top gear the Four would pull away smoothly and rapidly without snatch. Acceleration using the gears was rapid.

Charles Markham on the 1947 Four he christened 'The Gent' for the style in which it covered the ground

It was very easy to produce a 600 version of the revised four as reducing the bores to 50·4 mm gave a capacity fo 599 cc. While intended to appear with the one litre model, the smaller was only in the production range for one year in 1939.

That year saw the first introduction of the Ariel plunger rear suspension with constant chain tension designed by Frank Anstey. It was a rather complex link design that was to last longer than it deserved for the correct wheel arc was achieved only over too few inches of movement and was undamped. It was also prone to wear which did nothing to help the handling.

The sole purpose of the linkage was to move the wheel spindle in an arc about the gearbox sprocket centre, while the plungers worked in a straight line. Unfortunately this requirement was allowed to take precedence over the need to keep the wheel upright and true to the frame. In Europe it was common practice to link plunger springs to a swinging fork which could be braced to carry the wheel but this meant far more radical frame changes.

Anstey had a plunger with load and rebound springs attached on each side of the rear part of the frame. A collar was held between the springs to slide up and down and had a lug attached to it with a cross hole located aft of the spring. The pin in this was free to pivot and fixed to a short arm mounted horizontal. This arm carried the wheel spindle at its aft end and was connected to the frame by a short vertical link at the front. As the spindle moved the arm was forced to move in an arc by the presence of this link which coped with the required fore and aft movement. With three pivots on each side it was not surprising that wear was a problem.

That brought the Four up to the war and like the rest of the range it was dropped for the duration. When the conflict ended Ariel were very quick to return to production of civilian

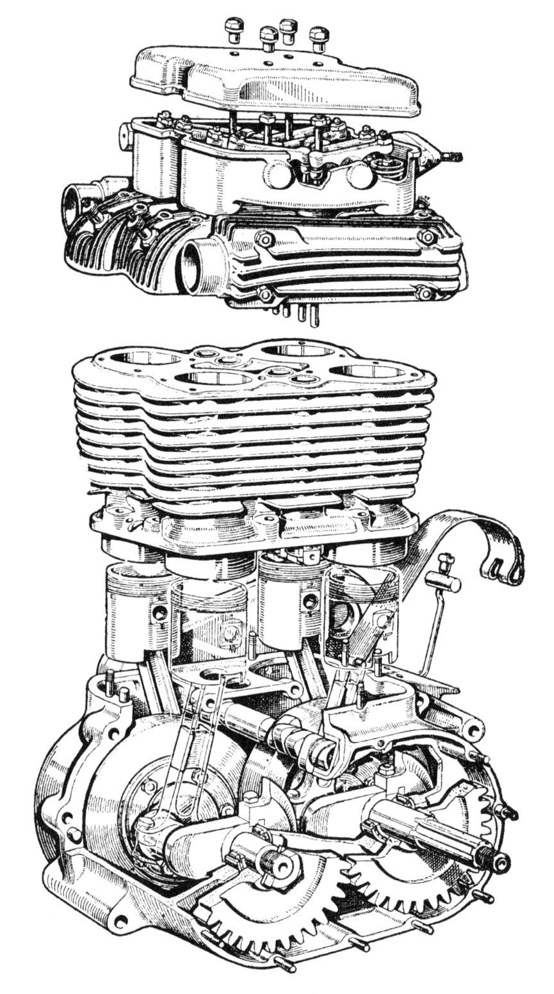

Above **Line drawing of the 1947 Square Four engine part exploded to show the compact nature of the assembly**

Far right **Advert from** *Motor Cycling* **dated 25th November 1948**

models, and announced their range in July 1945.

The Square Four was in it but only in the one litre size and in its 1939 form with rigid frame. The mudguards were extensively valanced and the instrument panel still set in the top of the petrol tank. It carried the speedometer, listed as an extra although a legal requirement, an oil gauge, a panel light which could double as an inspection lamp, and the quick action filler cap. Tubular silencers were fitted.

Like the other models the Four had a rear stand plus a front mudguard stay that doubled as a stand at that end. It was also fitted with a prop stand as standard, this being an extra for the others. The rear suspension system and telescopic forks were still in the future and no delivery dates were quoted for them, but the complete range was to be in production by October despite the presence of the military machines which were still being built in the plant.

At the time no mention was made of the immense difficulties all firms were having in returning to civilian production or the restrictions on material supply they had to work within. Long before the home market had received even a trickle of machines, the politicians were calling desperately for exports and most models went abroad. Few were allowed to stay in their own country and at first a permit was needed to purchase any machine. In time the hand of wartime bureaucracy was lifted, but by then the Government call was 'Export or die' and machines remained in short supply for some years.

Despite the problems progress was made and the news of the Ariel range was coupled with a picture of a Four fitted with rear suspension and the prototype telescopic front fork. One such model was also fitted with a dualseat, but that one belonged to Arthur Bourne—then editor of *The Motor Cycle*, and fitted with other non-standard parts.

In the middle of 1946 the telescopic forks were described in the press and fitted to the Four and the sports singles. Their design was elegantly simple and was to stand the test of time for two decades or more. The fork springs, in solo or sidecar rates, went above the oil seal holders in the legs and pushed against the lower fork crown. Oil was forced through cross holes to provide damping and a tapered stud in the foot of the fork leg provided a hydraulic stop on full deflection.

The lower fork crown had split lugs to clamp onto the fork tubes and carried the moving side

THE WORLD'S MOST Comprehensive SERIES
ARIEL
ARIEL
... THE Only RANGE
OFFERING SINGLE · TWIN
& 4 CYLINDER MODELS

1
2
4
ARI 111
ARI 222
ART 444
1 Red Hunter 350 and 500 c.c. O.H.V. "Super Singles" DE LUXE 350 and 500 c.c. O.H.V. and 600 c.c. S.V.
2 Red Hunter and De Luxe 500 c.c. Vertical model KH and KG—the Aristocrat of Twins—Spring frame at extra.
4 SQUARE 4, the 1000 c.c. with the astronomical acceleration—the Monarch of the Multis.

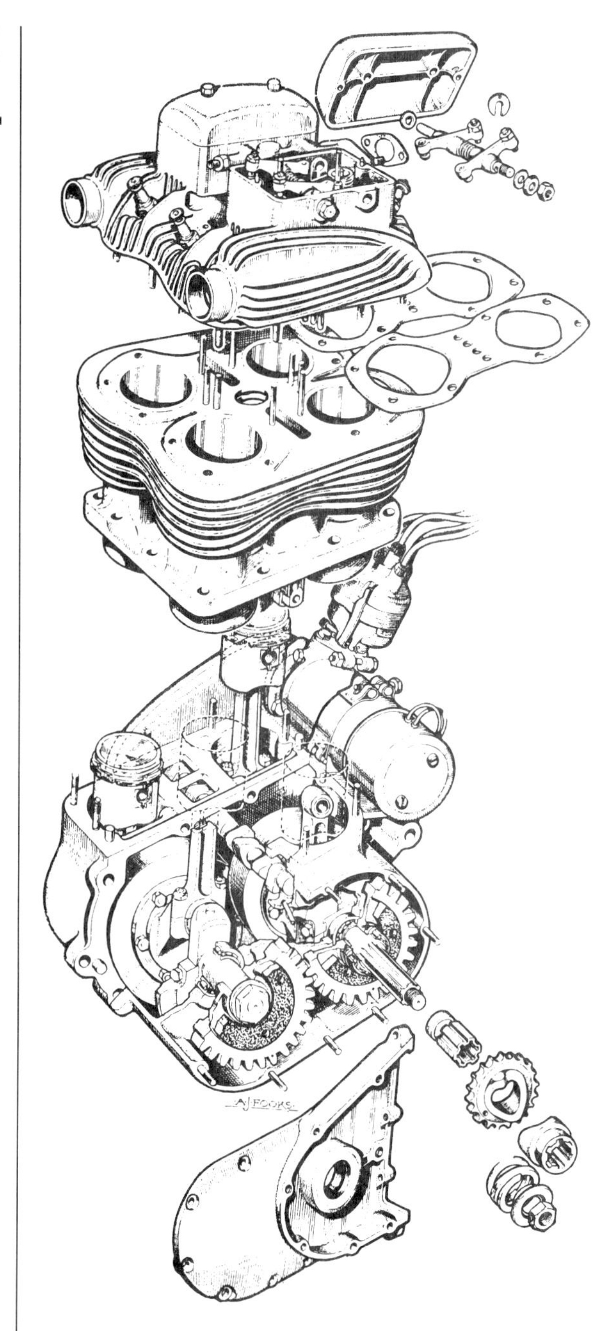

The 1949 all-alloy engine with coil ignition and cylinder head cast in one with manifolds and rocker boxes

of the steering damper, while the top crown pulled down to a collar on the steering column. Beneath it went two thin head race nuts on top of a dished washer, and these allowed adjustment to be made without disturbing the crowns while the washer gave the required preload to the bearing.

The front hub was new to suit the fork with a pull out spindle clamped up by a nut on the brake side. The other end of the spindle went through the fork end which was split, and a pinch bolt secured it. Thus it also dealt with any tolerance variations and the wheel was always located from one point.

The front brake was new although it did use an old, tried and trusted Ariel design from the rear hub and one they had adopted prewar. In this the brake shoes were cam operated in the usual manner but adjustment was at the fulcrum end of the shoes. The adjustor was threaded into the backplate with a square head on the outside and a cone with flats on the inside, these flats bearing on wedges which acted on the shoes. As the adjustor was screwed into the backplate the advance of the cone moved the shoes apart.

This design was used for many years prewar for the rear wheel which retained the usual wingnut on the end of the brake rod to compensate for chain adjustment. It was to be used for both for a good few years postwar.

There were no changes to the Square Four for 1947 and an article by Charles Markham, doyen of road testers until his tragic death, indicated why. In bald terms he reported on a road test machine that still did 94 mph despite some 30,000 miles in the hands of many riders, all determined to ride hard. He called the machine 'The Gent' not for what it did but the way it did it. Quiet, smooth and very pleasant to ride at all speeds it enabled Charlie to put up some very fast averages on the indifferent roads of the time by its ability to whistle up to a high cruising speed without effort. Hills it laughed at and, like all machines with capacity and a high gear, it

All-alloy Square Four of 1949 with link type rear suspension, still fitted with tank top instrument panel

The Anstey designed plunger and link rear suspension as used from 1950 with screw chain adjustors

covered the ground with ease. Fuel it drank at the right side of 50 mpg if the throttle was spared a trifle, which is what could be expected for the cruising speeds used.

1948 brought a change to a chronometric speedometer, but otherwise the model continued as it was except that the connecting rods were fitted with detachable, steel backed, white metal liners and the cap bolts were reversed to place their nuts at the top. Thus by removing the cylinder block it was possible, even if none too easy, to change the big end shells without dismantling the crankcase. At the same time the split pin locking was discarded in favour of locknuts.

The Motor Cycle published a road test in the middle of the year and returned a top speed of 89 mph obtained in a downpour with a fairly boisterous wind and the rider clad in bulky clothing. Such was the smooth spread of power that it was possible to pull away in top gear and the exhaust was very subdued. Unfortunately the engine was less so and thought to be sub-standard as one piston slapped and the crankshaft gears and valve rockers rattled.

The brakes returned good figures and helped

Above **1949: on the test bed for the 100 hour test**

Right **Another** *Motor Cycling* **advert for the Four, used on 16 March 1950 issue**

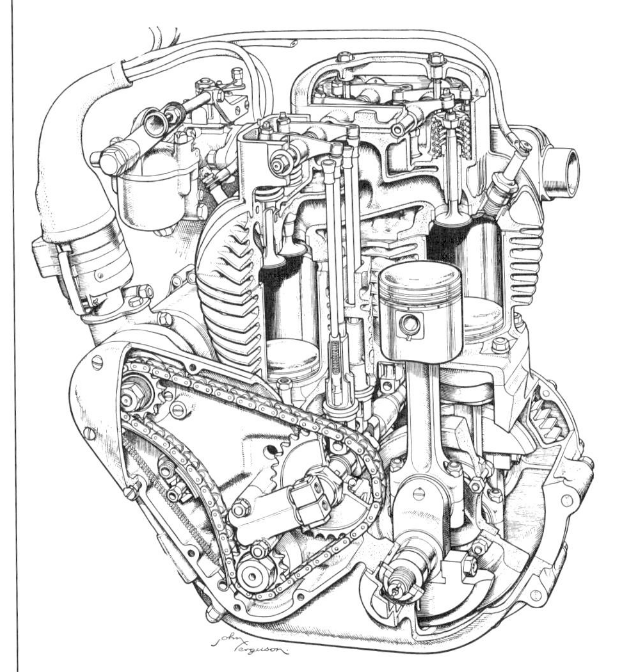

Line drawing of the 1949 engine showing the bolted flywheels and spring loaded tappets

the machine to achieve high averages despite having to retard a heavy machine. The test weight with some fuel came out at 476 lb which was a good deal above the original conception of a light, lithe model that Turner had set out to build nearly 20 years earlier.

For 1949 Ariel decided to do something about the excess poundage and the result was an all alloy engine which took 33 lb off. At the same time the magneto was replaced by coil ignition as service experience indicated that it was having a hard time running at engine speed. In its place went a 70 watt Lucas dynamo and skew driven from this a car-type four cylinder contact breaker and distributor with centrifugal advance and retard mechanism.

In its essentials the lower half of the engine was unchanged but the three cam lobe engine shock absorber was changed to a two lobe which gave a smoother power flow.

"MOTOR CYCLING,"
MARCH 16 1950
IN Spring A YOUNG MAN'S FANCY
TURNS TOWARDS ARIEL
and the joys of
the Open Road
Ariel "Leaders of Design" are the only British Manufacturers offering FOUR TWIN & SINGLE Cylinder Motor Cycles.
ARIEL MOTORS LIMITED, BIRMINGHAM, 29
ARIEL
ARI 444

The crankcase was modified so that the oil filter was central in the base of the sump and the timing chain tensioner modified to prevent it stretching out flat under stress reversal. The lubrication of the coupling gears was improved and the four ignition leads from the distributor plus that from the coil were contained in a weatherproof rubber moulding. The timing cover was altered in that the '1000' inscribed up to then was changed to 'Square Four'. Externally the steering lock increased, a new rear number plate was fitted and the front brake backplate was chromed.

The heart of the change for 1949 was the alloy head and barrel. The cylinder block remained in one piece and the four liners were a press fit into it. Four more holding down studs were added to make twelve in all, neatly arranged with four along each side. Unlike the iron block, the push rod tunnels were cast-in as two slots and the head gaskets no longer had special inserts for the push rod tubes, just a row of four holes for the rods themselves.

The tappet blocks were a push fit into the block and the tappets made in two sections with a spring between them to keep all the valve gear in contact at all times. As soon as the cam came off the base circle the two parts touched and worked as one.

The cylinder head complete with inlet tract, exhaust manifolds and two rockers boxes was cast in one in an aluminium-nickel alloy. The valve seats were in nickel-chrome steel and the inserts for the sparking plugs in bronze. Stylish fins ran across the tops of the exhausts and along their sides, while the pipes were held in place by finned clamps once more—plain ones having been used postwar up to then. The rocker boxes were cast into the top of the head with the inlet tract between them, and the oil feed piped into the exhaust rocker spindles. The four spindles were held in a cunning manner by a single nut on the outer end while they also pulled out the same way. This was done with a loose 'C' collar on the inside which located on the spindle to act as a flange.

The valves were without caps and each was restrained by two springs. The valve centres were changed slightly and the floors of the rocker boxes were sloped to assist oil drainage. Each was sealed by a lid secured by two sleeve nuts. The head itself was held down by a total of twenty fixings with eight of these being studs in the centre area with nuts, of which four lay inside the rocker boxes and four outside, while the other twelve were studs in the head held by nuts inserted between the cylinder block fins. Thus the head had to be held about $\frac{1}{2}$ in. up from the block while these nuts were started on their studs after which they could be run up, the bolts inserted, and all twenty carefully taken down.

The new engine had a very clean look to it thanks to the integral manifolds and with its red and chrome tank and rims many felt the machine to be the best looking Squariel of all. The spring frame was still an extra but few were sold without it. A very comfortable saddle was still fitted while a pillion pad and rests were available to order.

Early in 1949 the firm gave one of the new four engines a prolonged bench test to check wear and general behaviour. It was run in for ten hours and then given eighty hours at 4000 rpm on three-quarter load followed by ten hours at 5000 rpm and full throttle to make a total of 100 hours running time.

Motor Cycling road tested a four near the middle of the year and for them it was good for 92 mph while consumption varied between 40 and 50 mpg and was as directly connected to the twistgrip as the engine response. They found the riding position tiring over long distances due to the low seat height and wide tank, but as always the machine itself would cover distance quickly and effortlessly. Acceleration was rapid and quiet while the brakes hauled the machine to a standstill with ease. Roadholding was said to be impeccable but later writers were to be

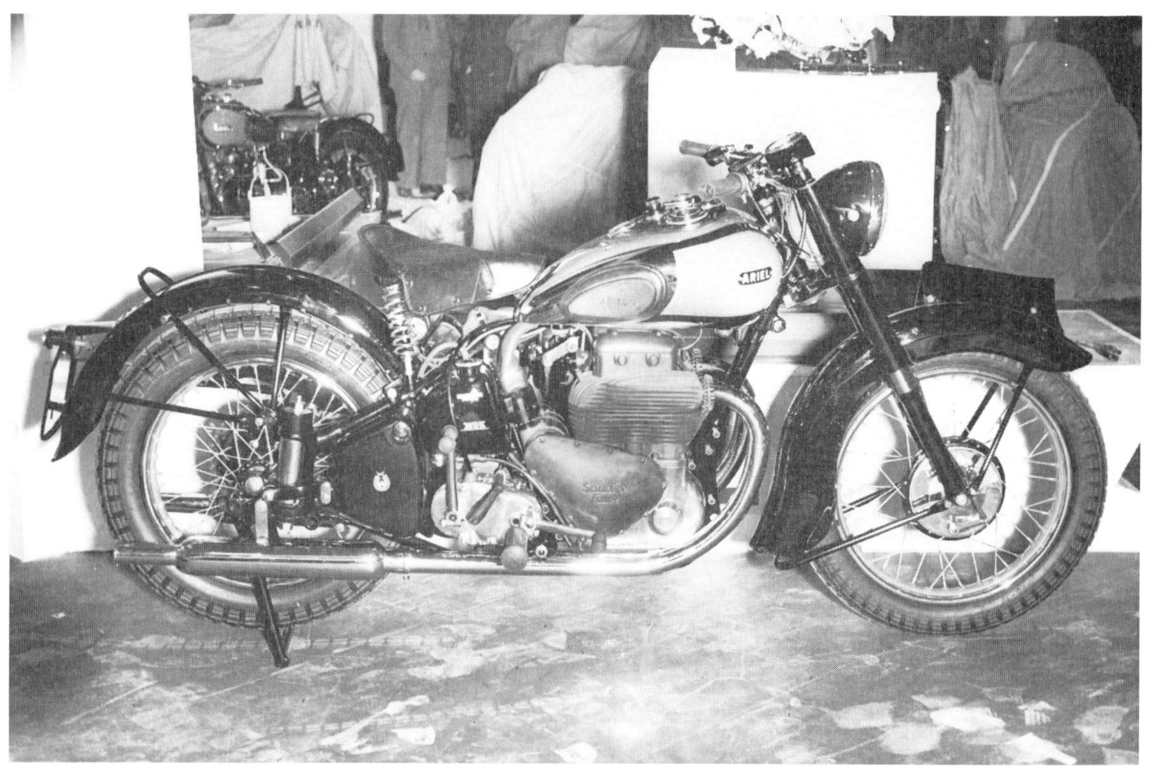

Above **A 1950 model waiting to go on show with speedometer in fork bridge**

Below **Line drawing of the Squariel as in 1951 with utility tank finish and pressed badges**

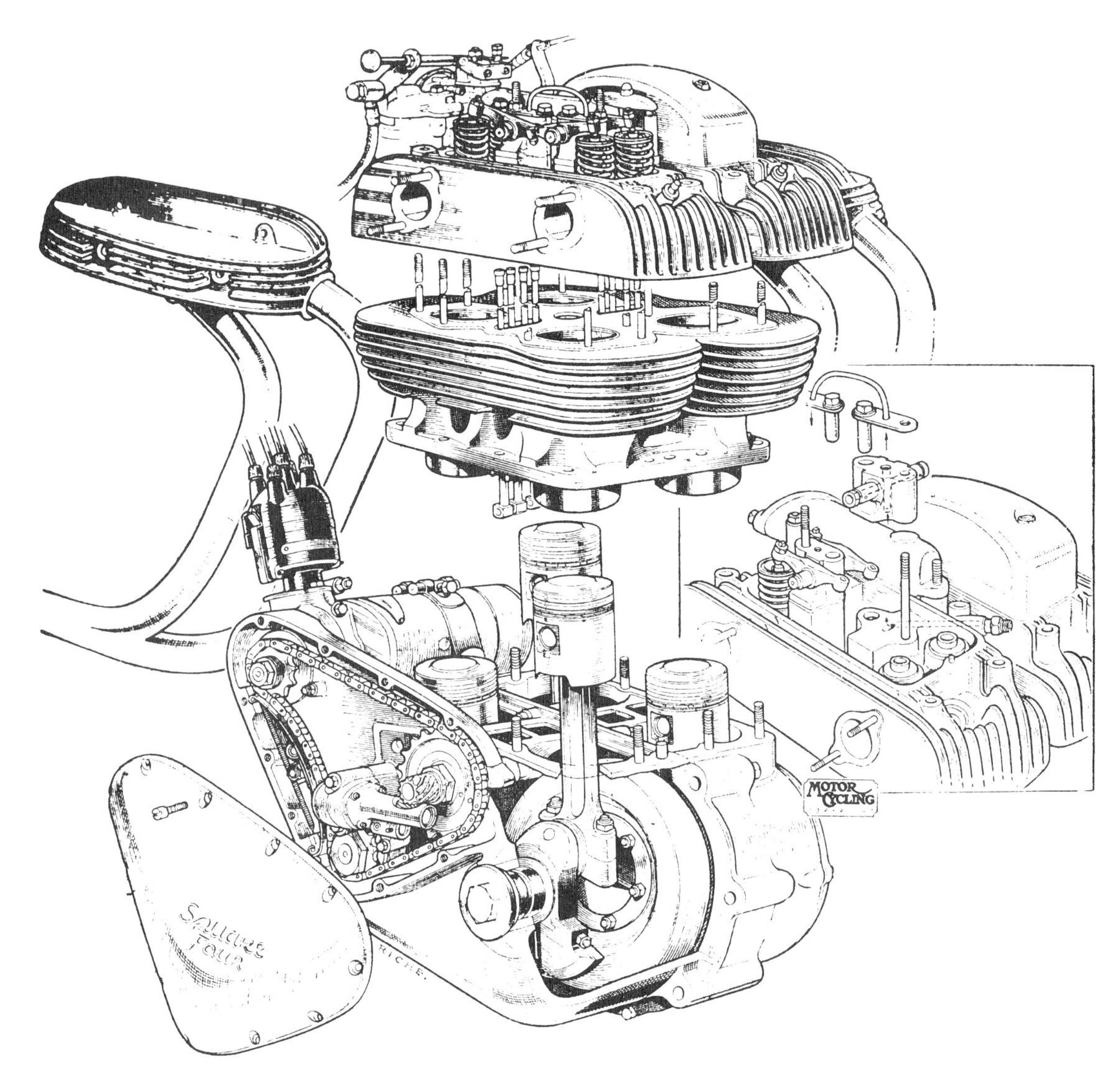

less kind to the undamped rear end which could allow the machine to pitch and weave over rough roads. For all that, it was adequate for the times and if you did have to slow a little more for the bends you had the pleasure of that scintillating acceleration to regain the lost speed.

For 1950 there were minor alterations one of which was to mount the speedometer in a bridge attached to the tops of the fork legs. It was thus much easier to read and any reduced access to

The four pipe Square Four or Mark II version introduced in 1953 with revised head and block plus separate manifolds

the light switch in the headlamp shell was removed by transferring that item to the tank top panel. An ammeter went into the hole left vacant by the speedometer and an ignition warning light was fitted between it and the filler cap.

A quickly detachable rear wheel was fitted as

standard, the mudguard stays changed from vee section to tubular, and the seat height raised an inch to improve the riding position. The rear brake pedal was modified so that its travel was not limited by it striking the exhaust pipe, and a pre-focus headlight and a new propstand were fitted. The appearance of the engine was enhanced by polishing the exposed areas of the crankcase, the base of the cylinder block and the edges of the cooling fins.

Early in 1950 *The Motor Cycle* had a four on test with a Watsonian sports single-seat sidecar. For this it was geared down and proved to be as fast in third as in top at 70 mph. For all that it was an exhilarating outfit to drive even if the test panel recorded a terrifying 52 ft for braking from 30 mph. Some excuse for this was the wet surface, while the report of squealing the front tyre under braking no doubt resulted in part from the narrow section and ribbed tread.

1951 brought a change in appearance as the tank top panel went and this increased the capacity a little. The top fork yoke became an alloy die casting which housed the speedometer, and both light switch and ammeter were moved back to a panel in the headlamp shell. The ignition switch went under the saddle which received barrel shaped springs, and the oil gauge remained in the tank top by itself apart from the filler cap which was moved into a central position ahead of the gauge.

The rear mudguard stays were changed and simplified, while a lifting handle was added, not before time, and the main part of the mudguard allowed to pivot up from under the saddle to aid wheel removal. The front number plate gained a cast fitting to surround it and give it a new style from the prewar form, while the battery strap was made wider, chromed and altered so that it would accommodate variations in battery size more easily. The battery capacity went up to 20 ampere hours and the rear brake was increased in diameter and width while its weight went down, thanks to a diecast alloy backplate.

Early in the New Year it was realised by the industry that they would have to restrict plating due to a shortage of nickel and in February Ariel announced that their tanks would be finished in red or black, gold lined and with a new, pressed badge. This continued into 1952 when the four received a petrol tank which was a little deeper in section and larger while the propstand was moved forward a little as it was for all the models.

During 1952 the gearbox was changed to the Burman GB which was of the same basic type but completely different in regard to the details. The layout followed English practice but the selector rods were extended to the right to a barrel cam fitted in the outer end cover and directly controlled by the foot pedal. The clutch continued dry and to live in a separate compartment in the chaincase.

The alloy engine was known as the Mark I and for 1953 it was joined by a Mark II version. This was better known as the 'four-piper' as the exhausts for the cylinders were separate and four in number. The main change was to the cylinder head which remained in alloy but with separate exhaust manifolds and inlet tract as in the 1937 unit. The exhausts were $1\frac{1}{4}$ in. diameter pipes which pushed into the manifolds and swept down to a common $1\frac{1}{2}$ in. pipe and tubular silencer.

The inlet tract was once again separate and bolted into place on top of the head between the two rocker boxes. While the cruciform tracts in the head were as before the size of them and the inlet was increased. The rockers were in the same position but each pair oscillated on an overhung pin in a central supporting block. The blocks were joined, front to rear, by an oil pipe and supplied under pressure as always. Sleeves around the valve stems, modified guides and chamfers on the tops of the rockers were all added to ensure that oil did not penetrate to the combustion chambers. As on the Mark I, the valve gear was enclosed by a pair of polished alloy covers, in this case held by two nuts. The

1953 Mark II with four exhaust pipes and sports front mudguard

head fixings were changed again to a total of fourteen studs screwed into the block and four bolts which went in from above to pick up their nuts.

Below the head went a block with slightly deeper finning containing split skirt pistons that gave a compression ratio of 6·7:1 for pool petrol but could be changed for some giving 7·2:1 if you could buy something a little better. Inside the timing case the oil pump was changed to a gear type with the pressure release valve in the body. It was driven by a worm on the end of the camshaft and the suggestion was made that the change gave a steady flow of oil instead of pulses. Curiously the Triumph engines managed to survive with plunger pumps while the new Ariel one looked very like that also employed by the parent BSA company for their twin. A further change was a small detachable sump plate and gauze filter added to the base of the crankcase.

Aside from the engine alterations the clutch inserts were changed to Neoprene to cope with the increase in power and the gearing was raised. A five gallon fuel tank was fitted, chrome plated as before for export. A new propstand was fitted and the rear brake operation changed to cable to ensure that wheel movement had no effect on the pedal operation. A Diacon stop and tail lamp was fitted at the rear and the dreadful underslung pilot at the front. At the front end the mudguard was more sporting without the large valance of that used for the Mark I, which continued in production.

For both models the rear suspension was still listed as an option but very few were seen without it. A dualseat option was said to be becoming available and the new four had a new colour of Wedgewood blue with white lining.

The four-pipe four was quicker than its predecessor and a test by *The Motor Cycle* returned a maximum of 97 mph. The machine was fitted with the Ariel dualseat which raised the riding position just enough to reduce the knee angle to a more acceptable degree. For the rest, it was the Squariel as before, pitching and weaving over poor road surfaces but offering the discerning, luxury performance.

During 1953 there was a move to fit Earles leading link front forks to the four and other Ariels and this programme very nearly reached

1953 Mark I has same cycle parts in general including underslung pilot and continued with oil gauge in tank top

production. The first indications were reports in the press of models fitted with these forks and also re-styled about the headlamp and with a larger twin leading-shoe front brake.

In April came a full description and the new forks comprized a main tube bent to follow the contour of the mudguard and braced by a second tube behind it. At their lower junction went a plate with three pivot holes to allow an easy change from solo to sidecar trail. Between the plates went the fork which had curved arms, pivoted on rubber bushes and was controlled by two spring and damper units. The front mudguard was unsprung and attached to the fork arms, being cutaway to clear the pivot.

At the top of the forks the main tubes were welded to the lower crown and the top yoke assembled in the normal manner with the head race adjustment beneath it. The whole of the steering head area was enclosed by a cowling which extended forward to carry the headlamp with a round pilot lamp beneath it. Mounted in the top of the cowling were the speedometer, light switch and ammeter.

The lines of the forks were quite acceptable and the handling generally good but one or two quirks appeared. At low speed the handling was heavy thanks to the sheer weight and inertia of the steering system, and under braking the front end rose because the torque reaction of the standard brake was taken by the fork arm.

Later on it was found that the handling deteriorated at high speed and the head races wore rather rapidly, while braking was not as good as with the normal telescopics in use. The final straws in the dropping of the idea were two deaths, one that of Ted Crabtree who was then Ariel's general manager and one of the men behind it, and the other that of Les Graham in the TT riding his 500 cc MV fitted with Earles type forks. Although nothing was certain as to the cause of the crash, the forks came under suspicion and fell from favour.

A new general manager had to be recruited and the choice fell on Ken Whistance and he set Val Page off in a different direction of suspension design to produce a frame with swinging fork rear.

Thus when the range was announced for 1954 the Mark III Square Four Royal Hunter, as the

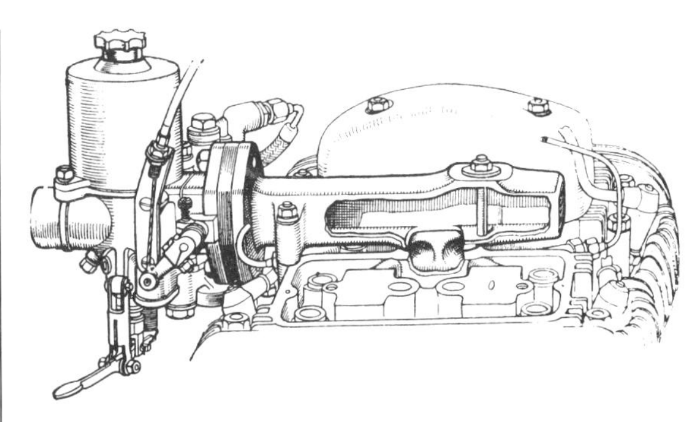

Above **The SU carburettor and extended inlet tract introduced in 1954**

Below **Nice outfit with 1954 four pipe doing its job of pulling a Watsonian Warwick two adult sidecar. Good for 77 mph**

Earles fork model had been called, was not in it. The new frame was used for much of the range but not the four which continued in Mark II form only with its link suspension at last fitted as standard, the Mark I model being dropped. The only real change for the year was to an SU carburettor, which necessitated a frame modification, and to the inlet tract. This had to change to accept the disposition of the carburettor fixings and the tract itself was lengthened to stretch past the vertical port into the cylinder head to avoid any mixture bias to the front or rear barrels. The compression ratio was made standard at the higher 7·2:1 and the finish was altered in line with the range to a round plastic tank badge, chrome plated tank flutes and a chrome band running

The fork cowl adopted in 1956 along with instrument panel, neat bar clamp and straight pull twistgrip

part way along the base of the tank side. The colour became black and the lining reverted to gold.

A *Motor Cycling* test carried out with a two-seater sidecar attached found that the additional power of the Mark II enabled it to reach a maximum of 77 mph. Thanks to the fitment of a side-car wheel brake the outfit was also able to stop in good order even when faced with a long steep descent into a town. Fuel consumption was well above 40 mpg so of an acceptable level for an outfit capable of providing a high standard of performance.

There was little change for 1955 with just the addition of a steering head lock set into the underside of the bottom fork crown, an integral

1957 model with full width front hub, enlarged oil tank and cross strap under headlight

Final form of 4G with valanced front mudguard, no forward stay and toolbox on left to make room for shaped oil tank

horn button and flexible fuel pipes. A deep claret finish was also offered.

1956 brought a change in appearance with a cowled-in headlight and full width, light alloy front hub. The cowl was rather short so the headlamp was set well back and the speedometer, light switch and ammeter were mounted in the top in a separate panel. A raised rib ran along the centre of the cowl top and the pilot lamp was set in the reflector. Handlebar appearance was further neatened by an alloy cap to clamp the bar in place, a combined horn push and dip-switch and a straight pull twistgrip.

The new front hub retained the pull-out spindle and, while the cast-in iron drum liner was the same 7 in. diameter, the shoe width was increased to $1\frac{1}{2}$ in. The brake shoes were light alloy as was the backplate and the adjustment system remained the same with a cone with flats screwed between the shoe ends.

Above **'No-one knows the troubles I've found'. A Mark II in the workshop**

Left **1959 Four with Steib sidecar, a very desirable outfit**

One further noticeable change was to the oil tank whose capacity was increased to 8 pints by extending the tank down and to the rear of the gearbox. It thus occupied all the space within the frame outline on that side so the toolbox had to be moved to the left. The colour continued to be deep claret only but the colour lining of the wheel rims was dropped so these became chrome plated only. The tank badge colours were changed from red and gold to chrome yellow and black with a chrome surround. Finally the gearing was lowered one tooth on the engine sprocket.

Early in 1956 a change was made to the timing chain which became duplex and endless. The ratio between crankshaft and dynamo was altered to 1:1·2 to speed up the dynamo so it cut in earlier and, to compensate, the distributor gearing was amended so it ran at the correct speed. This change was first introduced for overseas police work, but to assist production all models were built to the same standard. With the duplex chain came a hardened steel adjustable shoe to maintain tension and this replaced the Weller spring.

A further effect of the duplex chain was that it gathered up more of the oil in the timing chest and threw it at the breather outlet. This messy habit was cured by extending the breather pipe inside the case with a clip onto an oil pump bolt to support it.

Midyear *Motor Cycling* road tested a Squariel and on that occasion recorded a top speed over the ton at 102 mph. As always, the undamped rear end upset the high speed handling despite the efforts of the forks to keep matters under control. The new front brake was well reported on and in most other aspects the machine performed as of yore.

There were minimal alterations for 1957 and inside the only one was that the inner face of the clutch drum had Ferodo inserts rivetted to it to stop chatter. Externally the front mudguard lost its forward stay and was braced with a deeper valance and reinforcing on the underside. This allowed the then mandatory front number-plate to be mounted on the side of the mud-guard. The appearance of the headlight cowl was improved by the addition of a cross strap fitted under the lamp to the fork clamp bolts.

Which brought the Squariel to its final production form as it was to run on without further change. An instruction from the main group board halted development work so the Mark IV never came onto the market. This had the alloy engine in a more modern frame with swinging fork rear suspension and was a logical development, but only the prototype was built.

At the Ariel works the effects of these dictates from on-high were to have far reaching effects and an early one was the retirement of Val Page in January 1959 at the age of 67. He remained

Above **Interesting experimental Four with conventional rear suspension and heavy duty Leader trailing link front forks plus headlamp nacelle**

Below **The prototype Mark IV with alloy engine in swinging fork frame with late type front end and fittings**

in touch as a consultant for a while but with his departure various interesting projects came to a halt one by one.

Ariel were by then under the control of the main BSA group and subject to their decisions. They had a new model, the Leader, which was selling well and 1959 was a boom year for motorcycle sales. So they made a major decision to stop production of all the four-stroke models in order to concentrate on the two-stroke. Unfortunately, 1959 was the peak of the boom and was followed by a steady fall in sales over a decade with only one brief upturn.

With the scrapping of the four-stroke line the Squariel went, mourned by those enthusiasts who accepted the handling for the sheer pleasure of riding such a smooth machine with such acceleration. It was an expensive model but for those that could afford it the charm of wafting up hills and not having to flog the engine was worth it.

Two attempts were made to revive it. The first, in 1966, was an obscure effort in Canada with a scheme that included an increase in capacity to 1150 cc, overhead camshaft, fuel injection, electric starting and shaft drive. The rear brake would be a disc, but no mention was made of water cooling or any other measures to cope with the inevitable excess heat in the block. Nothing more was heard of this project.

The second had more success and came about when the Redditch-based Healey brothers, George and Tim, bought a sprint four in 1964. Before long they found they had to travel further and further to find spares so began to

The Healey 1000/4 in its early form with wire wheels and drum front brake. Egli spine frame with front tie-rod

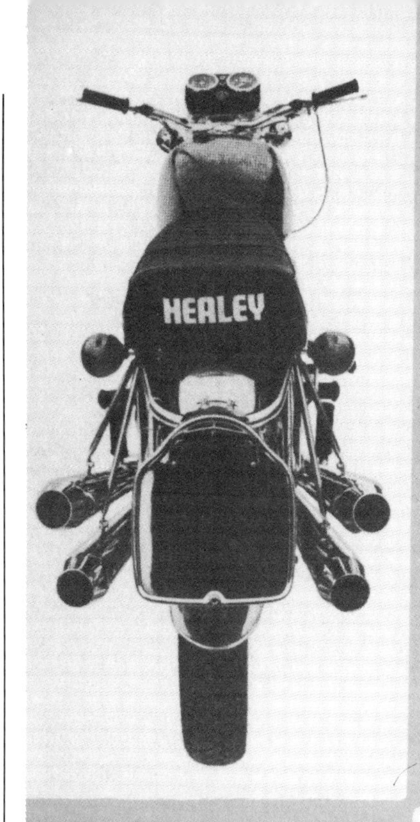

50 bhp at 6000 rpm, ten bhp more than the old Ariel "Square Four", and 80 lbs less in weight. It all adds up to performance.

The spine frame, race developed. No curved tubes, amazingly good road-holding, and an oil reservoir in its backbone.
A bike for riding. For the long distance men, whether basking in the bliss of coastal roads in high summer sun, or needing the security and faith of a trustworthy machine in mountain blizzards. The 1000/4 has it.

If Ariel had seen a decade hence at their decline, this is what they would have wanted, surely.

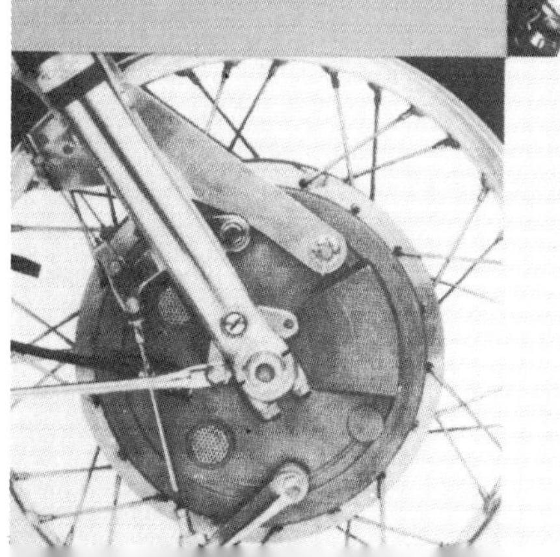

G. C. & T. Healey
Bartleet Road
Washford Industrial Estate
Redditch B98 0DQ
England
Telephone: Ipsley 3315

Healey in 1976 with cast wheels, disc brakes at both ends and stylish black exhaust systems with reverse megaphone silencers

make their own, and this soon led to them doing the same thing for other owners. So in 1967 they went into business as Square Four specialists and, in time, became involved with fellow Black Countryman Roger Slater, who was then building the Egli-Vincent. They had plans to make complete machines but were having trouble getting the frame as they wanted so Roger suggested adapting the Egli to take the Ariel engine.

The result was a spine frame Squariel with swinging fork rear suspension. The main spine tube doubled as the oil tank and supported the engine from above. At the rear went a tubular sub-frame on each side to carry the rear fork, the rear units, the seat and the rear engine plates which surrounded the gearbox. At the front a single tie bar joined the headstock to the front of the crankcase and this had a turn buckle adjuster in its length to make sure it held the engine up. The frame was plated as was the rear fork, while Metal Profile telescopics went onto the front end.

Healey catalogue indicating more power and less weight resulting in a return to the original lively performance. Detail of Egli spine frame interesting indicating ease of fitment to Square 4 engine unit

The engine had the lubrication system improved and an oil cooler added, but the transmission remained the usual Burman. The brakes were Italian drums with a duplex, twin leading-shoe assembly at the front, while the rear contained a further transmission shock absorber. Both wheels were wire-spoked and had alloy rims.

A rather humpy tank finished the machine off and initially the seat was short and had the appeal of a plank! The area beneath it was untidy as no side covers were fitted at that stage, but the instruments were neatly packaged in a console with an ammeter set between speedometer and rev-counter. Four separate exhaust pipes were fitted, each with its own reverse cone megaphone-style silencer, and these were all chrome plated and hung from chrome stays.

The first machine was built around 1971 and

Alternative special with Ariel engine in Norton featherbed frame

modified over the years. By 1973 it had gained a much improved dualseat, side covers, and a better tank finish but the splay of the exhausts and general lines of the machine looked wider than they really were.

The next change was to disc brakes at the front with hydraulic operation and by 1974 an alternator had been fitted onto the rear crankshaft. To accommodate this a dome was welded to the outer chaincase to clear the stator but the dynamo, with its drive to the distributor, continued *in situ*.

1976 saw the Healey 4 in its final form with cast alloy wheels and a single disc front and rear. The finish was altered with matt black exhaust systems and more styling to the tank decor. In the end it became too expensive to produce and so no more were made.

In its final form it was not too far removed from Turner's original concept—light, lively and exhilarating to ride.

3 The twins

Once Ariel had their peacetime production under way in 1945 with a line of singles and the four, they were able to turn their attention to the matter of twins. Like all the major English firms they had been left at the post by the 1937 Speed Twin from Triumph and Val Page may have felt this more keenly than most. He had after all been involved while at Ariel with a 250 cc twin concocted from the rear half of a Square Four fitted with a 360 degree crankshaft and suitable camshaft. Whether it was he or Turner who were responsible for this exercise is open to debate but Page was the senior man at Ariel even if the four was Turner's special baby.

Page went on to build a twin for Triumph in 1933 and must also have been involved with the two experimental twins built by BSA in the late thirties. Certainly the line of the timing cover of one was very similar to that of the later Ariel.

After the war all the firms needed a twin urgently to match the Triumph, and Ariel had a couple of advantages. First was the existence of cycle parts which could take the size, weight and power of the four, so they had the option of using single or four items in the chassis and knowing it would all work. Second was the initial design study Page had carried out during the war so they had a prototype running late in 1944.

The twin was first publicised late in 1946 when it was pictured at a Brands Hatch grass meeting and by that time it had run up an impressive development mileage and been tried by several

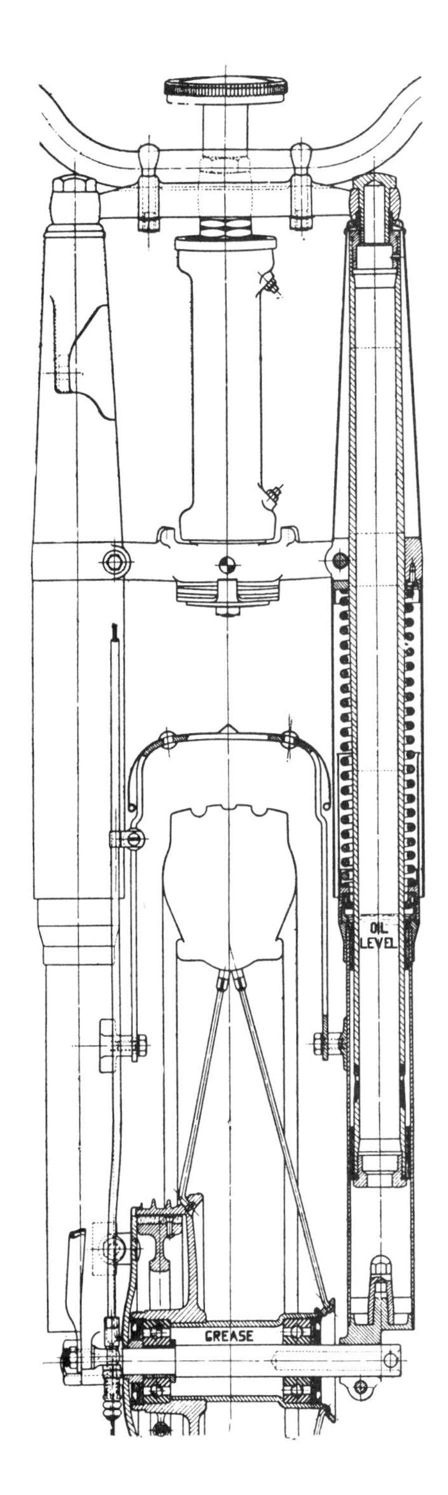

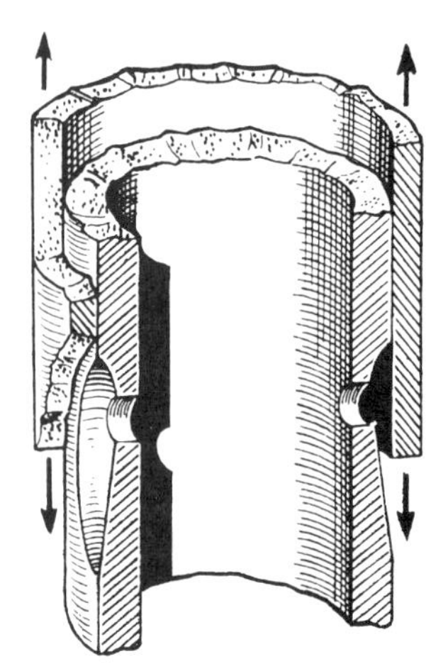

Above **Detail of oil port**

Left **Cross-section of the Ariel forks introduced in 1946 and used by the whole group**

press writers to gain their comments. During 1947, as the firm struggled to get back to normal production in the face of many problems and shortages, more twins went through their paces in the hands of different riders from both trade and press. They liked it.

The twin was not among the models listed for 1948 when the programme was announced but in November 1947 a full description was given in the press. With this came the news that it really was twins as two models were announced, the KG500 de-luxe and the KH500 Red Hunter, the second a little more sporting than the first.

The engines of the two models were virtually the same with the Hunter model producing a little more power thanks to a higher compression ratio, polished cylinder head and bigger carburettor. Both were based on dimensions of 63 × 80 mm and thus copied the Triumph with a capacity of 499 cc. Compression ratios were 6·8:1 for the KG and 7·5 for the KH and the general engine construction followed English convention for the time but with a number of interesting points that Page considered improvements. Thanks to pool petrol the compression ratio for the Hunter soon reverted to that of the

Ariel advert announcing the advent of their twins in Red Hunter and De Luxe forms

de-luxe but the higher domed pistons remained available as an option.

The heart of the engine was the crankshaft which was a one-piece forging to which a central flywheel was bolted. This gave a number of advantages in rigidity and accuracy over the build-up type and the only snag was the need to find a forger with heavy enough equipment to do the job. Given that proviso the single forging was much cheaper to make.

The crankshaft had a balance weight formed in each outer web and a round flange formed between the crankpins to take the flywheel, which was secured by six bolts. The one problem this assembly brought was that of threading the flywheel into place and to allow this to be done its inner flange had two cutaways and an easement. Fitting it into place was akin to a Chinese puzzle but no problem at the works or, outside them, to those who had the crib.

The crankshaft ran in two main bearings, the timing side one on the right a white metal lined, phosphor bronze bush and the drive side a roller bearing. End float was maintained at the bush using a thrust washer and shims to suit. The mains went into a vertically split crankcase which extended well up to support the top half of the engine. The two halves were dowelled and spigoted together with a ring of studs to secure them including two in the crankcase mouth.

The connecting rods were forged in RR56 light alloy with split big ends fitted with white metal lined, steel backed shells. The big end bolts were a tight fit in the caps with a locating diameter at their midpoint and were secured by locking nuts. As on the four, the purpose was to allow the shells to be changed through the crankcase mouth without the need to split the case halves.

The small ends had bronze bushes and the pistons ran on light, hollow gudgeon pins retained by circlips. Each piston was a light alloy hot pressing, oval ground, and fitted with one slotted scraper and two compression rings. The crowns were slightly domed with valve recesses cut into them.

The cylinder block was a one-piece iron casting held to the crankcase on eight studs. Both bores were spigoted down into the mouth to support the pistons and each spigot was slotted fore and aft to clear the connecting rod. The push rods went at the four outer corners of the block with tappets below them so the air flow between the bores was unobstructed and the cooling fins even and unbroken.

The cylinder head was cast in iron complete with its four rocker boxes. Air was able to flow freely between the boxes and extra holes between the fins ensured that there were no dead pockets of hot air trapped anywhere. A copper-asbestos gasket went between head and barrel and the two were joined with eight studs screwed into the underside of the head. The studs had plain extensions to pick up the nuts which went between the barrel fins and this method of attachment avoided studs and holes running through the head in awkward points.

The porting was a single inlet with flange at the rear which fed the two cylinders and exhausts sited well out on the corners of the head with a degree of splay. Each rocker box was open at the top with an angled face and this allowed the assembly of the pressed in guide, valve, duplex springs, collar and retaining split collets. A cross hole took the rocker spindle, and on these oscillated straight line rockers with a pressed in ball end on the inner side.

The outer end of the rocker was threaded and fitted with an adjuster which was locked by a cross screw closing a split on to its thread. Both adjuster and cross screw had Allen heads so the toolkit contained a hexagon key to turn them. The four rocker boxes were closed by a pair of lids, each held by a single sleeve nut which screwed to a stud in the head. The lids were cast in light alloy and were louvred to allow air to flow between the rocker boxes.

The timing side of the engine was as straight forward as the rest. A duplex sprocket was keyed to the end of the crankshaft and connected by

Exploded line drawing of the twin engine with details of head fixing, tappet adjustment and crankshaft lubrication

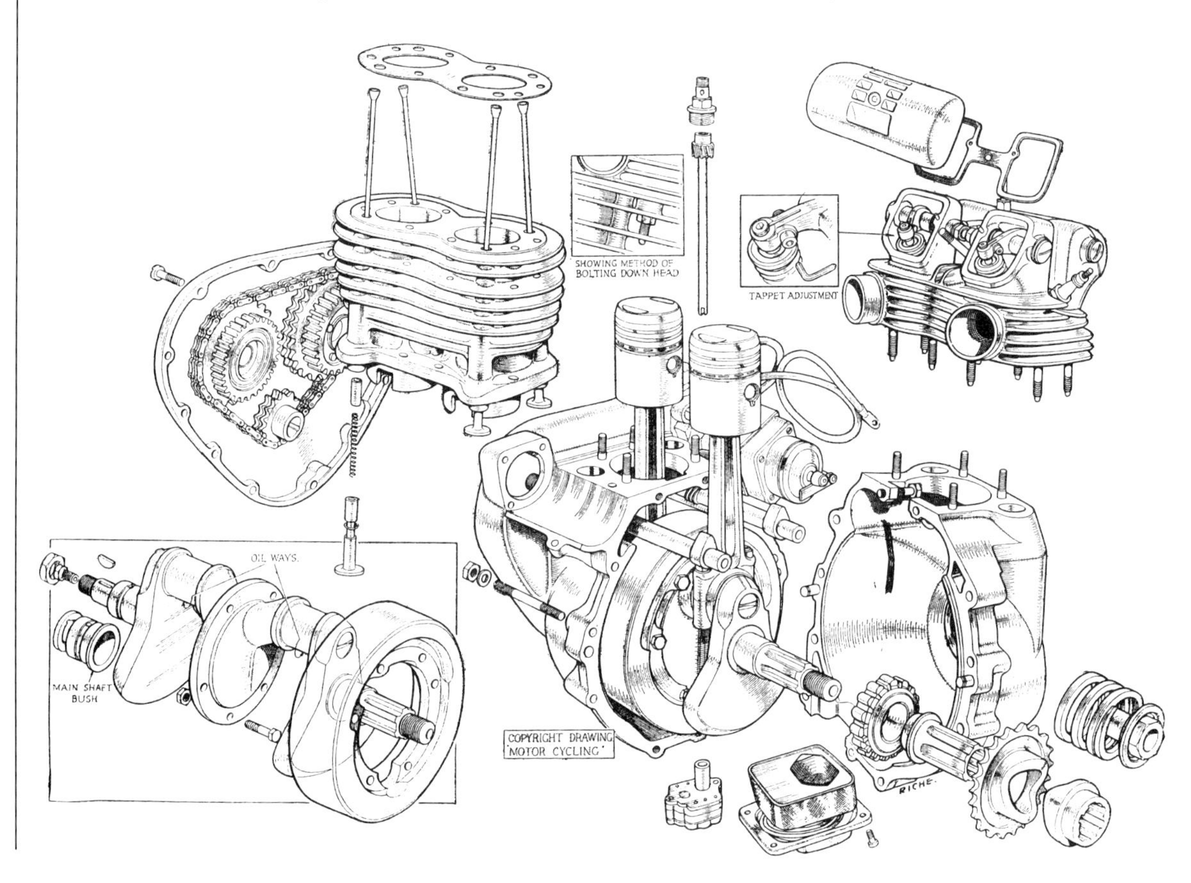

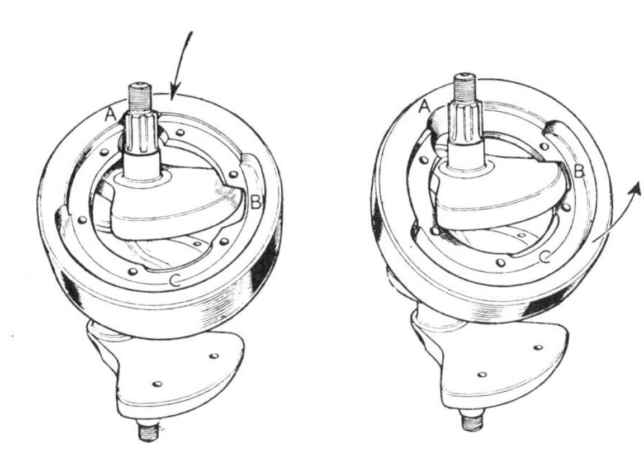

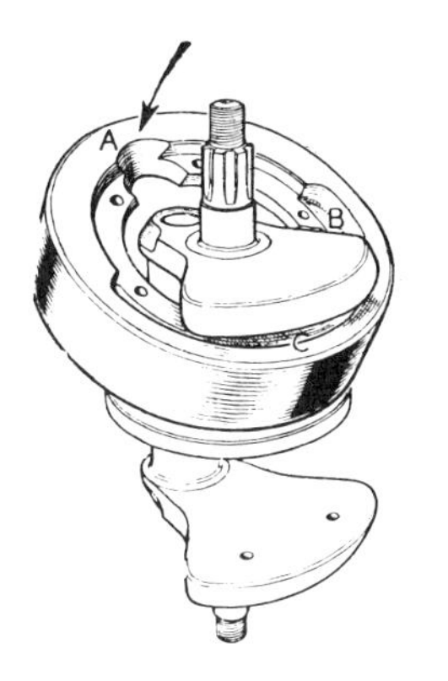

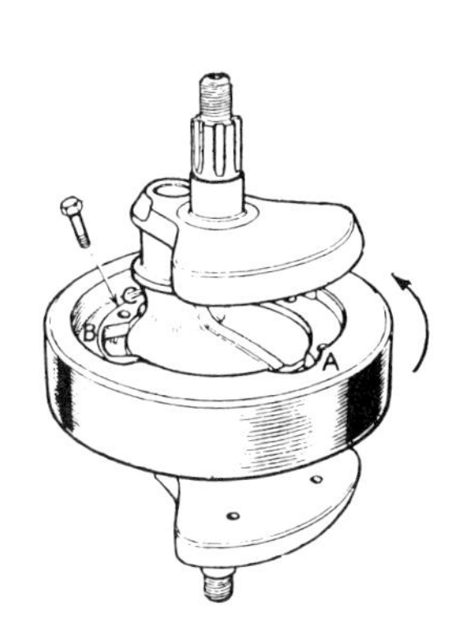

How to thread a flywheel which had slots and easements to allow it to pass over the crank webb

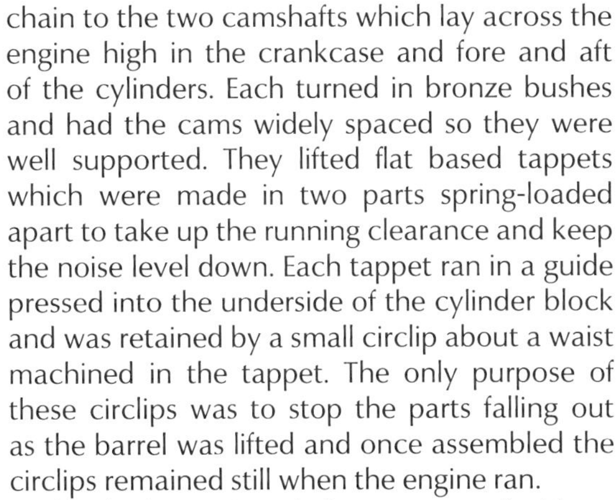

chain to the two camshafts which lay across the engine high in the crankcase and fore and aft of the cylinders. Each turned in bronze bushes and had the cams widely spaced so they were well supported. They lifted flat based tappets which were made in two parts spring-loaded apart to take up the running clearance and keep the noise level down. Each tappet ran in a guide pressed into the underside of the cylinder block and was retained by a small circlip about a waist machined in the tappet. The only purpose of these circlips was to stop the parts falling out as the barrel was lifted and once assembled the circlips remained still when the engine ran.

The duplex timing chain was controlled by a Weller tensioner on the slack run and the movement of this restrained by an adjustable stopper plate. The timing chest was formed by extending the crankcase to front and rear and these extensions served to accommodate the electrics which were gear driven from the camshaft sprockets.

At the rear went a Lucas or BTH twin cylinder magneto and fixed to its armature was a steel gear incorporating a centrifugal advance mechanism. This meshed with a Tufnol gear which was riveted to the back of the inlet camshaft sprocket. The drive at the front was not quite the same as the Tufnol gear was not riveted to the sprocket but held to it by a domed spring steel washer which allowed it to slip if overloaded. This gear was meshed with a steel one fixed to the end of a 6-volt Lucas dynamo that was clamped to a machined recess on the crankcase top front. The entire timing side was enclosed by a single alloy cover of triangular shape secured by a row of screws around the edge, and at first this was plain but very soon gained the legend 'Ariel Twin' in its centre, later shortened to 'Twin'.

The lubrication system was dry sump but departed from Ariel practice by using a gear pump rather than a plunger. The reason was a preference for the steady output it gave rather than the pulsating one of the plunger, this being considered better for the plain bearings. The oil pump was located at the base of the crankcase and driven by a vertical shaft with a gear at its upper end which meshed with a worm cut on the inlet camshaft. The pump was enclosed by a wire mesh filter held up against it by a coil spring located by a detachable sump plate. By removing this and the filter the oil pump could be easily taken out if required.

The oil tank was connected by lines to a pair of pipe unions set in the rear of the right crankcase half. The pump supplied oil directly to the timing side bush and thus into the crankshaft which was drilled so that it passed to both big

Below **The 1950 Red Hunter twin with speedometer on fork crown and other common cycle part changes for the year**

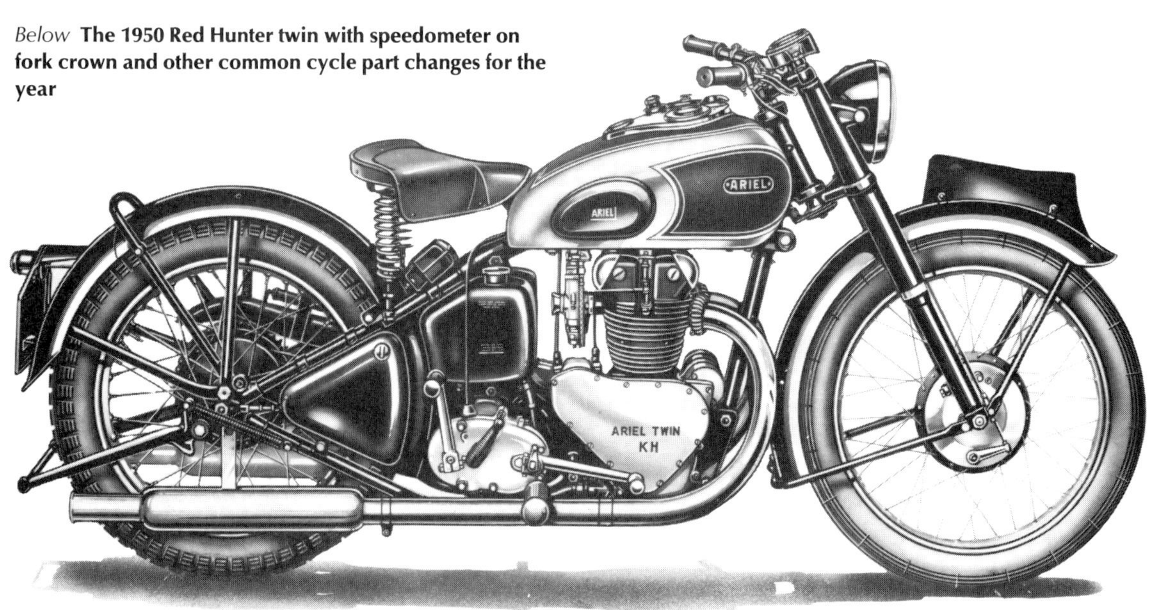

Left **The 1948 Red Hunter twin in its rigid frame as introduced without finned exhaust pipe clips**

end bearings. The exit hole was at a point nearest to the crankshaft centre to help equalize the oil feeds and reduce the effects of centrifugal force. Set in the timing end of the crankshaft was a simple pressure release ball valve.

A subsidiary feed was taken by an external pipe running up the rear of the block to a five-way junction between the rocker boxes. Four of the ways connected to a rocker spindle and the fifth to an oil gauge. The oil from the valve gear drained down the push rod tunnels, over the cams, to the sump where it was scavenged. Just above the oil pump shaft an oil breather was fitted into the top of the crankcase and a banjo carried any outgoing oil onto the rear chain.

A single Amal with float chamber on the left looked after the intake, and on the outlet side there were pipes clipped to the exhaust stubs with tubular silencers on each side of the machine. The carburettor choke was spring-loaded, so dispensing with a lever on the bars and a cable. The weight of the complete engine with accessories was 98 lb and thus heavier than the single, but only by one pound.

The transmission of the twins followed the lines of the single with a two cam lobe shock absorber on the end of the crankshaft, single strand chain to Burman gearbox, and a dry clutch in its own compartment in the alloy primary chaincase. The gearbox was the type CP with four speeds and footchange and the final drive chain went on the left. Both solo and sidecar ratios were offered by a change of engine sprocket.

The cycle parts of the twins were nearly a direct copy of the singles but the frames did differ as the front down tube was pulled forward at its lower end to clear the dynamo on the twin. The link type rear suspension was offered as an option and the new telescopic forks went at the front. For the rest it was the same wheels, mudguards, tanks and toolbox with a valanced rear guard for the KG de-luxe model and no valance but a larger diameter front wheel for the more sporting KH Red Hunter.

The new twins had a nice line and early tests showed them to be fine machines. *The Motor Cycle* ran a de-luxe in both solo and sidecar forms with top speeds of 78 and 62 mph while *Motor Cycling* reached 93 mph with a Red Hunter. The first of these tests commented on the frequency with which the brakes needed to be adjusted and that the exhaust pipe limited the travel of the rear pedal so that this adjustment was fairly critical. Both magazines returned very acceptable braking figures which indicated efficient stoppers. The machines had a clean and tidy appearance assisted by the lack of advance or air levers and cables, while the bright finish—especially for the Hunter model—was most pleasing.

There were few changes for 1949 for production was the name of the game with customers clamouring for every machine that the makers could roll off the end of the line. Many machines were scheduled for export, especially the more interesting, so there was no incentive to alter except to eradicate faults that even the press of the times had vilified, cut costs, or add some cosmetic change at minimal expense.

To their credit Ariel did more than this for they read the road tests which had criticized the steering lock and modified the forks with new crowns to improve this. They also fitted the longer Lucas dynamo with improved output and lowered the gearing a little. On the cosmetic side there were finned exhaust pipe clips and a polished front brake backplate, both items which did enhance the machine's looks.

The gearing change was more far reaching than appeared at first sight as both engine and gearbox sprockets were altered and the gearbox type also changed to the heavier BA unit.

This carried the two machines on to 1950 when the tappets became one piece because owners failed to close up the two halves when setting the clearance. Thus they were left wide and 'clattery' like horseshoes over cobbles, and this did not sit well with the thoroughbred image the models had. This air of being elegant tourers was something they were never to completely shake off, although the machines were comparably fast to their contemporaries and the performance of the Red Hunter sporting. Perhaps they did their job in too quiet and smooth a manner to be thought fast or to fit the image the customer was looking for of proud, high-handed stallion or skittish mare needing to be mastered.

There were a number of other changes common to the range that year with the speedometer moving to the fork crown, the seat height up an inch, tubular mudguard stays, a new and

The Ariel horse in a typical advert for a twin in the early 1950s

deeper petrol tank with twin taps, and a new headlight unit from Lucas. The rear brake pedal was modified so that it always cleared the exhaust pipe, which meant that someone had read the road test, and there were options offered in the form of a quickly detachable rear wheel, ribbed front tyre and air cleaner. There was also a colour option in green for the KG.

1951 brought some changes in appearance with the fork top crown becoming a die-casting into which the speedometer was fitted. The ammeter and light switch went into a small panel attached to the headlight shell and thus the tank top instrument panel was dispensed with. In its place was an oil gauge fitted behind the central filler cap and the tank capacity went up to 4 gallons.

Further back, the rear mudguard stays were simplified and a lifting handle added, while the detachable mudguard tail was no longer used as most of the guard could be pivoted about a point beneath the seat to aid rear wheel removal. The saddle springs became barrel-shaped, the front number plate gained a cast alloy surround and the battery clamp was made wider, chrome plated and fitted with two clamping bolts to enable it to fit alternative size batteries.

Inside the engine the flywheel weight went up by 20 per cent and externally the fins of the head and barrel were made deeper. The exhaust pipe run was altered for aesthetic reasons and the rocker box covers to make them more rigid, and in the process they lost their cooling slots. On the timing cover the legend was changed to 'Twin KG' or 'Twin KH' as appropriate.

Early in the year the tank finish of the twins was changed due to the nickel shortage and, like the four, they became painted, lined and fitted with a new, pressed badge. Later on the fabric driving gears attached to the backs of the camshaft sprockets had a material change to Millenite soft iron and at the same time the slipping clutch in the dynamo drive was discarded. A further engine change was to the rockers where the clamp screws were dropped and conventional adjuster screws and locknuts were fitted.

When the 1952 range was announced the KG de-luxe twin was absent, officially to aid production efficiency, but more likely for the simple reason that customers preferred the Hunter. This

1951 de luxe twin, the more touring of the two models which was dropped from the range that year

continued with a new shape to its oil tank and just the legend 'Twin' on the timing case, while the propstand mounting was moved forward a little.

During the year the lubrication of the inside of the engine was improved by the provision of a shallow groove along the big end journals around the oil holes. This allowed more oil to flow out under pressure and so reach the other parts. About the same time the cam form was altered and with this came a change to the valve clearances. Finally, there was a change of gearbox which was phased in during 1952 with the introduction of the Burman GB type, also known as the B52 when used by other companies.

The next phase in the twin story came at the ISDT selection tests held in the middle of the year where three Ariel twins appeared fitted with light alloy cylinder heads and barrels. The result for the road was a similar engine in the Red Hunter frame for the 1953 range. This was the model KHA and the engine was based on the KH bottom half with the crankcase mouth modified to suit the new top.

The cylinder block was cast in a silicon alloy with the push rod tunnels and the iron liners were pressed into place and retained by top

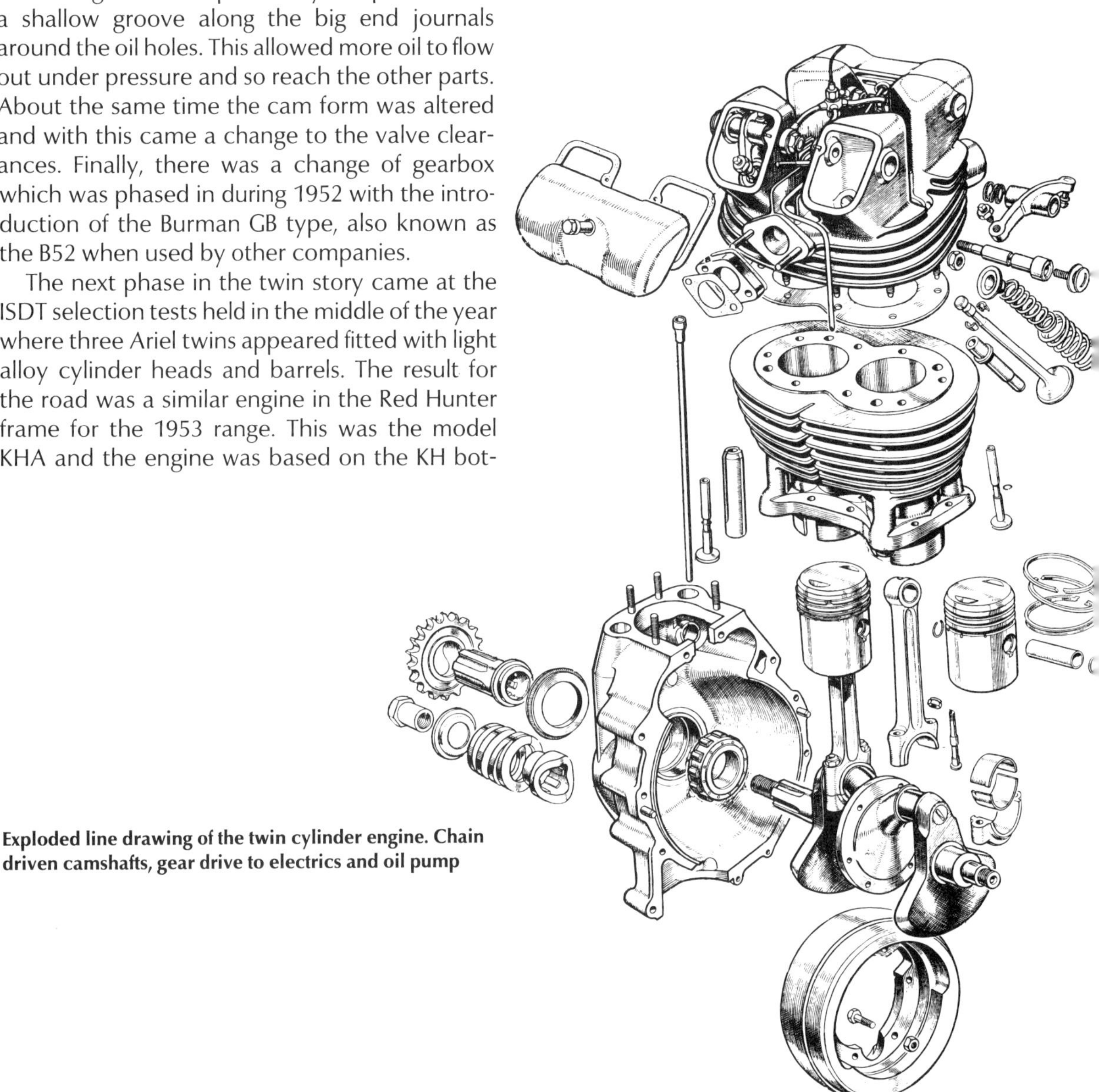

Exploded line drawing of the twin cylinder engine. Chain driven camshafts, gear drive to electrics and oil pump

flanges. The head had four separate valve pockets with the tops at a much flatter angle, as this permitted the push rods to be inserted after the head was fitted to the engine. Each well had its own lid secured by a pair of nuts and the push rods were in alloy with hardened ends.

The top half was held down by one central stud in the top of the barrel and eight special long bolts which screwed into bronze inserts in the underside of the head. These bolts had double hexagons low down to give more spanner positions when being tightened and were held to the crankcase by steel sleeves which screwed into its top. Thus only the stud loaded the barrel casting in tension.

The compression ratio remained at 6·8:1, although a higher option was listed for those who could buy better quality fuel. The cams had quietening ramps and the timing case legend was 'Twin KHA'. The remainder of the engine, and in fact the rest of the machine, was a repeat of the KH.

Both models were fitted with a cable rear brake when the link suspension option was taken up, a new propstand, underslung pilot lamp, and Diacon rear lamp. The new alloy model had the option of a dualseat and was finished as standard in Wedgwood blue with white lining and

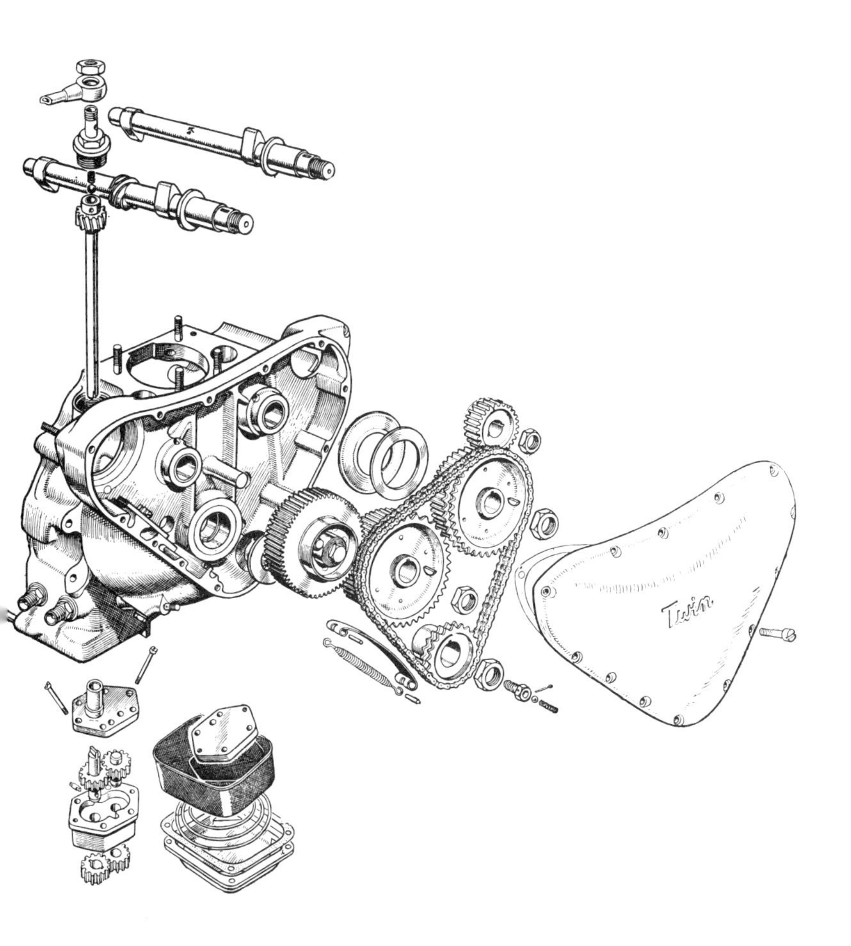

Above **The 1952 twin with painted tank against the off-white press photo sheet background**

Below **Someone's favourite Ariel with reversed cylinder head and added enclosure**

matching wheel rims. The export ones also reverted to chrome plating on the tank.

During the early part of 1953 the twins were involved with the Earles fork exercise along with the four and, like that model, the leading link variant was withdrawn before it reached final production. The exercise also produced new names with the twin called the 'Hunt Master' and the four the 'Royal Hunter'.

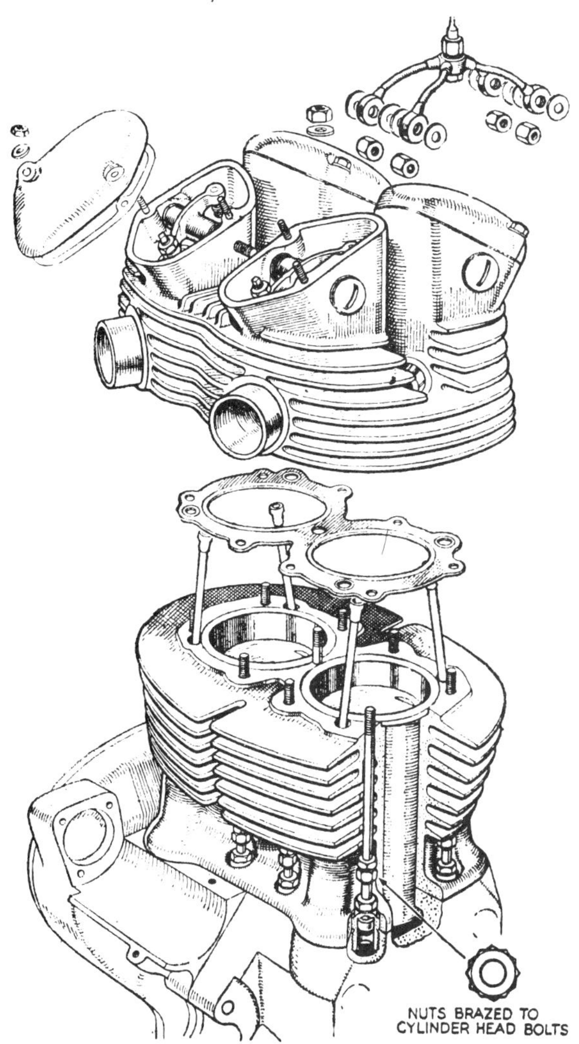

All alloy engine with through bolts anchored to crankcase and different form of rocker boxes

A road test of the all-alloy twin showed it to be good for a level 90 mph when equipped with pistons giving the optional 7·5:1 ratio to take advantage of improved fuels. Consumption was rather heavy at 72 mpg at a steady 30 mph and the natural gait of 70 mph was avoided due to a vibration patch. Because of this the machine was cruised more often at 75 mph which resulted in no ill effects. The brakes continued to work well and the gearchange was good as was the handling, except over bumpy roads when the undamped rear end induced pitching.

1954 was a year for changes as the all alloy model KHA was dropped, the KH well modified and a new twin, the 650 cc model FH, added to the range. The new twin, together with the 500 cc model, had a new frame with swinging fork rear suspension, a dual seat and revised ancillaries.

The new engine was in reality a clever group exercise in styling disguise for the unit was the A10 BSA with minimal changes to hide this fact. No mention of the basis of the engine was published at the time but the descriptions in the press were fairly brief. Engine dimensions were 70 × 84 mm so the capacity was 647 cc and the compression ratio 7·25: 1, this being the optional figure for the Golden Flash. In a short time the Ariel was altered to the standard figure of 6·5: 1 as used by the BSA, but naturally the optional pistons remained available. In fact there was little to stop the really determined from fitting the alloy head, hotter camshaft, manual magneto and 8: 1 pistons from the Road Rocket.

The engine followed convention in many ways with the crankshaft forged in one piece with integral bobweights and a bolted on central flywheel. It turned in a vertically split, aluminium alloy crankcase on mains with a caged roller race on the drive side and a plain timing side bush. The connecting rods were forged in light alloy with separate caps held by bolts with location diameters and secured by nuts, while the bearing surface was provided by indium flashed big end

The model KHA with all-alloy twin engine only built for 1953. Offered in Wedgwood blue with white lining

shells. Bushed small ends were used as were bored gudgeon pins retained by circlips.

The cylinder block was a one-piece iron casting held down on studs screwed into the top face of the crankcase. The push rod tunnel was cast-in at the rear between the cylinder bores, and the barrel was surmounted by an iron, one-piece head. This had the inlet manifold cast into it to carry a single Amal carburettor and both inlet valves sat in a single well with duplex springs retained by a collar and split collets. On the exhaust side there were two separate valve wells and the head fins encouraged the air to flow between these and then out over the combustion chambers and past the angled out sparking plugs. The exhaust pipes were a push fit onto the port stubs and carried finned clips.

On top of the head went a one-piece rocker box in light alloy and in this area there was a small change from the BSA item. The casting continued to support each pair of rockers on a single spindle but differed in respect of the rocker covers and the addition of an access hole in the top surface. This was provided to assist assembly as the A10 was difficult in this respect and required the use of a special comb to hold the push rods in the right position as the rocker box was lowered into place. The access hole allowed them to be pushed into the rocker cups and checked. The rocker covers differed only in being held in place by a single central sleeve nut screwed to a fixed stud rather than by four nuts as on the BSA.

The valve gear utilized a single camshaft running in bushes set in the crankcase to the rear of and above the crankshaft. It was gear driven by a pinion on the crank which meshed with an idler and then the camshaft gear. The cams lifted tappets which ran in the block and were retained by locking screws. The push rods ran from the tappets to the rockers and these had adjustors with locknuts at their outer ends.

The timing side gear train was extended to a further gear behind the camshaft and this drove a Lucas twin cylinder magneto via an automatic advance mechanism. The dynamo was clamped to the front of the crankcase and chain driven from a sprocket carried on the outer end of the idler gear shaft.

Further work for the timing side was done by it driving a timed rotary breather from the camshaft gear and, although this turned in the inner timing cover, it exhausted from behind the drive side main bearing housing. In addition, the duplex gear pump for the dry sump lubrication system was driven by a worm screwed to the end of the crankshaft. The pump was mounted low down on the side of the crankcase and the worm also held the timing pinion in place.

The timing cover was in two sections, inner and outer, and isolated the dynamo drive, which was grease lubricated, from the rest of the gear train. The inner cover was the standard BSA part but the outer one was special to the Ariel and of a different shape. With careful tailoring it lost its usual BSA form of two arms extending from a central area and became the rounded corner triangle associated with Ariel, and remarkably similar to the cover used for the 500 twin.

The lubrication system was straightforward with the supply taken from the external tank to the pump from where it went via a pressure release valve to the crankshaft. The rockers were fed from an external line connected to the return pipe and oil dropping from above dealt with the cams and tappets. This supply was augmented by the provision of a cast trough into which the cams could dip and which was maintained by the drain from the timing case. The oil finally drained into the base of the crankcase where a small sump plate held a gauze filter in place to protect the pick-up pipe which supplied the scavenge pump.

The transmission of the 650 was BSA at the front, and thus little different from the Ariel. The crankshaft carried a splined sleeve on which turned the sprocket. This was driven by a twin lobe cam which splined to the sleeve and was held in place by a heavy coil spring retained by a locked nut.

A single strand chain drove the clutch of the Burman GB gearbox and this area was Ariel for the separate compartment in the chaincase and dry operation was retained. The differences were that the A10 used duplex chain and the clutch had two less teeth than usual for an Ariel, 42 in place of the otherwise universal 44.

The KH engine was revised by fitting the alloy head to the iron barrel using the fixing method devised for the all alloy motor. The opportunity was taken to raise the compression ratio to 7·5 : 1 and the power output went up to that of the alloy unit. Otherwise the KH remained as before but with the legend 'Twin 500' on the timing case, unlike the 650 which carried the single word 'Twin' or sometimes the words 'six' and 'fifty' with a larger 'Twin' between them.

Both engines went into a completely new

The 650 BSA twin engine used by the Ariel FH with minor changes to timing cover and rocker box

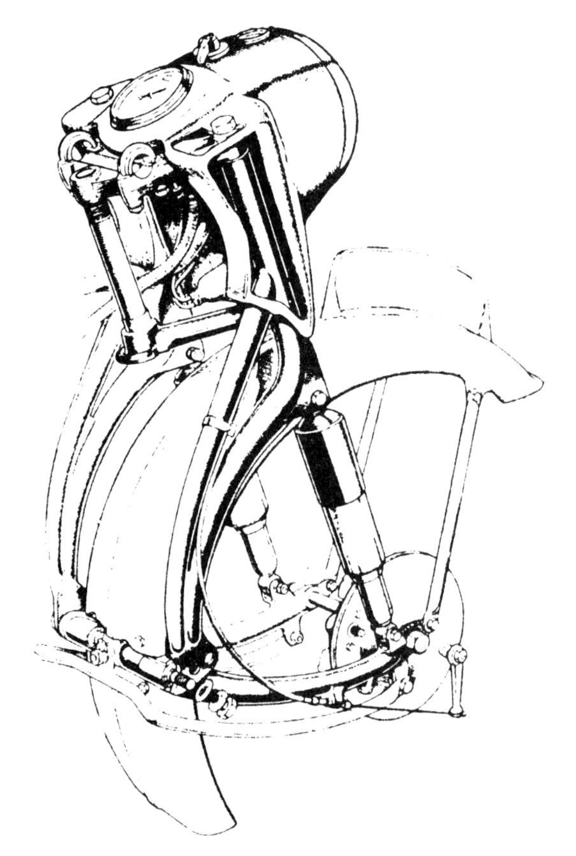

Line drawing of the Earles leading link front forks that reached their own catalogue but not production

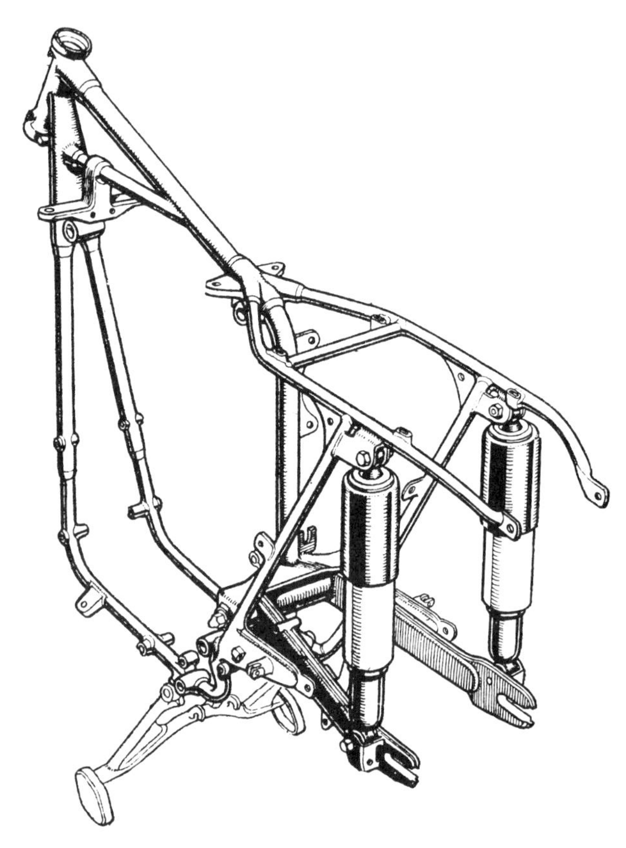

Swinging fork frame with duplex down tubes introduced for the twins and singles for 1954

frame of both brazed and welded construction. The headstock was forged and carried twin down tubes which turned under the engine and ran back to the seat tube before turning up at an angle to run to the top mountings of the rear units. A single top tube was braced to the headstock by a tube set beneath it and this carried the front tank support. The top tube terminated at a lug from which the seat tube dropped and two seat rails ran back to the rear units and beyond to support the rear mudguard with a single cross brace. The seat tube was cross connected to the frame loops and further braced by a sheet steel bracket which supported the rear fork pivot.

The rear fork arms were built up from pressings with a tubular cross member into which were pressed bonded rubber and steel bushes to provide the fork bearing. Fork movement was controlled by Armstrong hydraulically damped spring units and at the front went the usual Ariel telescopics. Pillion rests were attached to brackets welded to the frame, while the footrests bolted directly to the lower run of the loops. These also carried lugs for the prop stand and the centre stand which had elliptical feet for an easy roll-on action.

Due to the use of the new frame, many other parts had to be revised and a dualseat was fitted as standard. The oil tank was tucked neatly into the right sub-frame loop with a toolbox matching it on the left with the battery in front of it and the horn below it. Ahead of the oil tank and more to the centre of the machine went an air filter.

The petrol tank was re-styled with chrome plated flutes on the upper shoulders while the oil gauge went and the rear mudguard had a valance and a boxed-in rear number plate. The hubs and brakes remained as before and the machines were finished in deep claret with gold lining. The tank decor included a deep chrome band which ran back to the kneegrip on each side with the new round badge centred on its upper edge.

Late in 1953 one of the new 650 twins, which was also known as the Huntmaster, was used for a revised form of the Ariel sevens test. This was less complex than the prewar Maudes attempt and only involved the one machine which was fitted with a sidecar. The outfit carried a crew of two plus an official ACU observer, and the plan was to cover some 1700 miles through seven European countries in seven days. And, despite fog, ice and torrential rain, this was precisely what they did.

A Huntmaster was tested by *The Motor Cycle* early in 1954 and by then the rod rear brake had been changed to a cable. Under poor conditions and with the rider wearing bulky clothing a speed of 96 mph was reached with 89 and valve float coming up in third. The machine was overgeared for maximum performance but on the road this gave it a restful feel and it could run happily in top most of the time.

The new frame proved to have rather soft suspension and while this soaked up the bumps when travelling in a straight line, it was underdamped for cornering. The riding position was cramped and the dualseat too soft with a forward slope. the addition of two inches of sponge-rubber made a considerable improvement to riding comfort and confidence.

In May came news of another long distance test using the 650 and a sidecar. The idea was to ride right round Britain starting from the Mersey Tunnel in Liverpool. The Huntmaster was driven by Titch Allen and, due to his involvement with Feridax at the time, it was fitted with many of their accessories. These included a screen with

The Huntmaster 650 cc twin as introduced for 1954 with BSA engine in new Ariel frame and finish

apron, legshields, luxury dualseat and pannier set. The sidecar was a Nicholson saloon with trailing arm suspension and a braked wheel which could be operated by the rear brake pedal or independently by a handlebar lever.

The run started from Birmingham where it was to return after the circuit, and the climax of the test was to be a speed run at Silverstone with the sidecar removed. The aim was 500 miles in the same number of minutes.

The trip started well, but around the Scottish West coast the weather was poor and the serpentine roads gave Titch plenty of work to do. The rear chain broke near Dundee and by Lincolnshire a new rear tyre was needed. Titch also had several spokes fracture and near the end the sidecar spring unit lower anchorage broke. This was first replaced by a piece of wood sawn to fit in a local farm, and later by a new unit. The ACU observer who had travelled throughout in the sidecar received the blame for that episode!

Despite the problems, the trip was completed

Line drawing of rear chaincase and complex rod, bellcrank and cable operation for rear brake

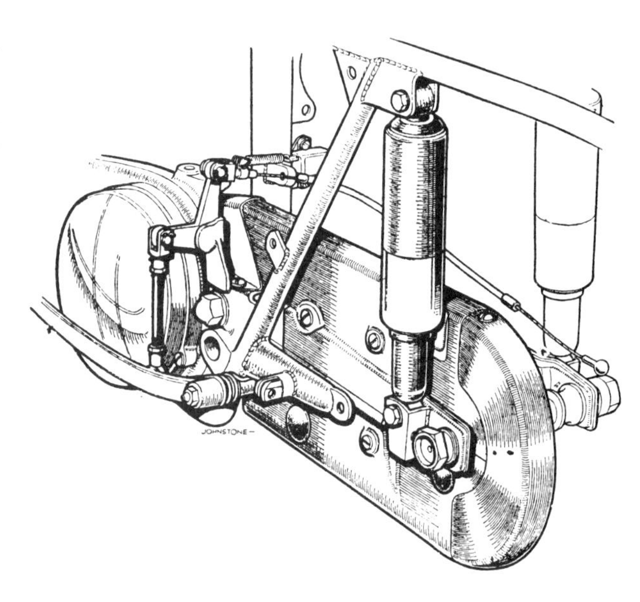

The 1955 KH Hunter twin with alloy head and iron barrel

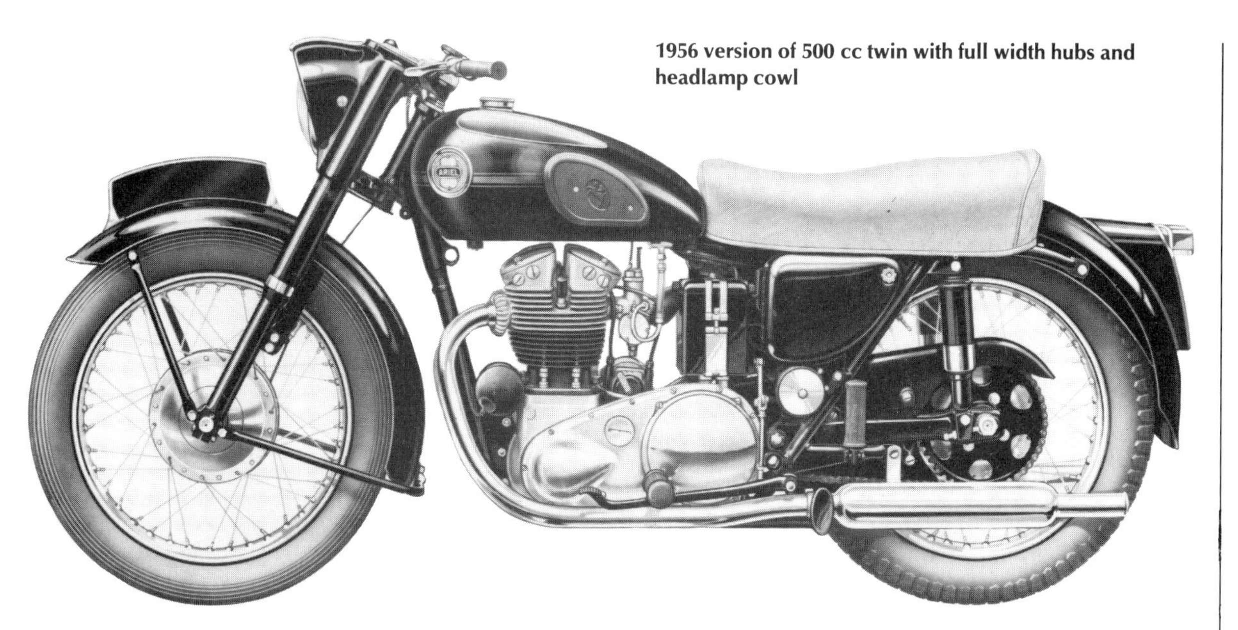

1956 version of 500 cc twin with full width hubs and headlamp cowl

on time after which the party repaired to Silverstone, but not before the engine was stripped and examined. It proved to be in a fine order except for one part, the plain timing side bearing which appeared to have suffered from the passage of a piece of grit or metal that had machined into the bearing.

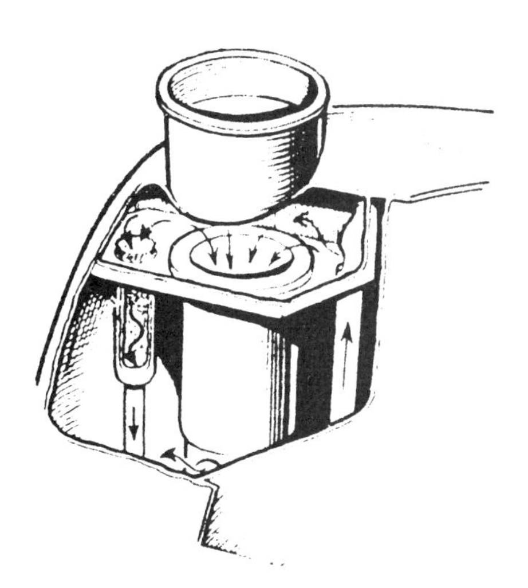

Revised oil tank with some returned oil allowed to seep through felt feed and thence to rear chain

The bush was replaced and the machine circulated the track for just over 8 hours to cover the 500 miles, finishing minus the oil tank cap, with the centre stand grounded, and with a dry rear chain. One stop had been needed to clear a blocked jet and five for rider changes.

As the test had come to a successful conclusion Ariel entered it for the Maudes Trophy, which had been with BSA since 1952, but were not awarded it.

1955 saw detail changes to the twins rather than radical alterations. In the engine there were chrome plated top rings for longer bore life and on the outside the Amal Monobloc replaced the old type 6 and was supplied via a flexible fuel pipe. On the sides of the rocker boxes of the 500 went small access holes with blanking screws to allow the valve clearances to be checked more easily without removal of the lids.

The lower fork crown was fitted with a steering lock, the oil tank filler cap was moved to the top front corner of the tank so as to be more out of the way of the rider's leg, the rear mudguard was extended and a longer rear brake pedal fitted. A screw-in horn button was used and the

Earls Court in November 1955 and visitors examine a cut-away Huntmaster

front rim and tyre size changed to 3·25 × 19 in.

In the middle of the year the camshaft chain tensioner in the 500 was altered. The new type comprised a hardened steel curved blade which pivoted in the timing chest at its leading edge. It was adjusted with a wedge under the trailing end which was slid back to tighten the chain and then clamped down by a single locked nut.

Motor Cycling tested a KH Hunter during the year and for them it returned a top speed of 89 mph and cruised at 70 plus. It was quiet and easy to handle with the brakes working well, despite the front being a little spongy. The rear chain oiler worked a little too well at first but adjustment cured the problem. The oiler had been an Ariel feature for many years and comprised a bleed from the primary chaincase which was controlled by a needle valve and directed by a pipe onto the rear chain.

For 1956 this arrangement was altered to accommodate a new optional rear chain case. The new scheme employed a wick set in the top of the oil tank which supplied a tube running down to the chain. The chaincase was not totally sealed as the front end was fixed to the frame and gearbox and the rear assembly to the fork. Tongue and groove joins were used in this and

The FH in its final form as built from 1957–59

it overlapped the front section with a small clearance and an arc about the fork pivot. Rubber plugs gave access to the chain for inspection, and to the nuts which held the quickly detachable hub to the sprocket.

Both hubs became full width, light alloy with a cast iron liner. The front was as used for the four and the rear matched it in appearance and design with suitable changes to provide the drive. The rear brake operation was by a rather complex rod and cable mechanism. The brake pedal was connected to a vertical rod with an adjustable fork end screwed on each end. The upper one connected to a bell crank which pulled on the cable inner with the outer located into a lug on the frame. In turn the cable ran to the rear brake backplate where an adjuster was provided. With this system, movement of the rear wheel to adjust the chain had no effect on the brake setting.

As on the four, the twins were fitted with the new headlamp cowl, with the speedometer, ammeter and light switch mounted in a panel at the top of the forks. The underslung pilot light was replaced by one in the reflector and the handlebars held by a clamp with concealed fixings. A combined horn button and dipswitch were fitted. The KH became known as the Fieldmaster, while internally the oil feed to the rocker boxes was reduced. For the 650 the recommended sidecar gearing was lowered a little.

Late in 1955 *The Motor Cycle* tested the Huntmaster and squeezed it up to the level 100 mph. All told, they seemed to like the model so much so that they re-tested it early in the New Year with a Watsonian single-seat saloon sidecar attached. This pulled the top speed down to 70 mph but it remained a zestful machine and the wide spread of power made it easy to ride quickly.

In March 1956 the tank flutes were made separate so that they could be chrome plated and then attached. This was done using three curved spring steel tongues which slid under strips

The Ariel Cyclone as exported in 1958 with high bars, sports mudguards, Spitfire camshaft and high compression pistons

welded to the tank. Sealing compound went round the edge of the parts and thanks to this change the tanks only required to be painted. This arrangement went for 1957 when a new tank was introduced. This was a little larger in capacity and sat on four rubber pads with a central single bolt fixing. This was concealed by a chrome plated strip which ran along the tank, clipped to the back and held by two screws at the front. The finish was also altered with smaller kneegrips on alloy surrounds and a single line on the tank shoulder.

Like the four, the FH had anti-chatter Ferodo facings rivetted to the clutch drum face and the gearing was lowered by making the clutch sprocket common to the rest of the range. On both twins the cross strap was added to the headlamp cowl and the front mudguard changed to a deeply valanced one without a forward stay. The front number plate went onto the valance and the prop stand gained a pedal to make it easier to swing out.

At the end of 1957 the 500 cc Fieldmaster was dropped, which brought the true Ariel twin to an end although the BSA ringer continued. It was unchanged for 1958, aside from a black option for the colour. Later in the year a red and black option was added to the two existing colours and these all continued for 1959 with no mechanical changes.

This was hardly surprising for the new Leader had been introduced in 1958 and the decision taken to concentrate on this model. Thus, at the end of 1959, the Huntmaster officially went, along with the other four-strokes.

The 650 did in fact run on into 1960 as the Cyclone for the US market and used the big bearing BSA crankshaft, Spitfire camshaft and high compression pistons. Finish was typical export with high bars and chrome plated mudguards and colour was red for the oil tank, tool box and petrol tank which had a black top section.

4 Working singles

At the end of the war the sturdy Ariel singles went straight back into civilian harness. With the war department 350 still in production it was easy enough to run a demobbed version alongside it, and then again easy to expand this single machine into a range.

For convenience this comprized five models from the 1939 lists with a de-luxe and Red Hunter model in 350 cc and 500 cc ohv sizes plus the 600 cc model VB with side valves for the sidecar man. Code letters were NG for the 350 cc de-luxe and NH for the more sporting Hunter, while the 500 cc versions were the VG and VH. The prewar 250 cc Hunter model was not continued with, to some people's regret for it was a model that gave good performance and light weight.

The four overhead valve singles were very similar in design but differed in the details. Thus the NG used the WD frame with its extra ground clearance and also its oil tank, while the others had the normal clearance under the duplex engine rails and a larger oil tank. The mudguards of the VG and VB were valanced, unlike those of the de-luxe 350 and either Red Hunter. Petrol tank sizes also varied with the 350s carrying less but all were fitted with the instrument panel as on the Square Four.

All models had girder forks and rigid frames as the rear link suspension was not then available. Further variances occurred with the silencers, for the side valve VB had a Brooklands shape with fishtail while the others had tubular units. All the overhead valve models could be had with a two port head and either type of head with normal or upswept exhaust pipe and silencer. There was a note that there could be a delay in supplying the machine if such items were ordered, which must have killed the demand stone dead in those days when new machines of any sort were at a premium.

The basis of all the models was the well proven Ariel single engine which dated back so many years. It might have been old but this only served to show how right the design had been in the first place. Engine dimensions were 72 × 85 mm for 346 cc, 81·8 × 95 mm for 499 cc, and 86·4 × 102 mm for 598 cc and thus neither bore or stroke was common to any other model.

The design of the bottom halves was identical with vertically split light alloy crankcase with the two parts spigoted together and held by a ring of bolts and studs. The flywheels all differed due to the various strokes and piston weights which affected the balance, but in addition the Hunter models had steel wheels in place of the cast iron of the others. The 500 cc Hunter also had a parallel crankpin and double row caged roller big end bearing, unlike the others which retained the two rows of rollers but left them uncaged. They also had a taper crankpin which was pulled up by nuts, and the same construction was used for both mainshafts in all models.

A very useful feature of the timing side flywheel was the sludge trap set in the rim. The lubrication hole in the wheel ran from the centre out alongside the big end pin and on to the periphery where it was blanked by a bolt. The effect was that any debris that managed to find its way past the filters and into the crankshaft was thrown by centrifugal force to the end of the drilling before it had a chance to change course into the big end supply hole. To enable it to be serviced the crankcase had a sump plate on the underside of the timing half and removal of this and the gauze filter it supported enabled the sludge trap bolt to be removed and the recess cleaned out.

The connecting rod was forged in steel with a hardened race pressed into the big end eye and a bronze bush in the small end. The piston was conventional and in 1945 the poor fuel available limited the ohv compression ratio to 6:1,

The side valve Ariel single VB600 built for many years with minimal changes. This is the 1938 model, 1945 virtually the same

The 1945 ohv single VG500 with girder forks used in those early postwar months

Early postwar advert for the NG350, a model with some differences from the NH and VG

while the side valve engine was on 5:1. Alternative ohv pistons giving 7·5:1 were to be listed but such dizzy heights were not to be reached in the austere Forties.

Above the crankcase mouth the two engine types differed with the VB barrel held on four studs and cast in iron with a valve chest in the side. Guides for valves and tappets were pressed in and single springs controlled the valves and were held by a collar and collets. The tappets were flat based with screw adjustors at the top and the exhaust carried a washer that the valve lifter worked against. The valve gear was totally enclosed by a finned cover which was held by a single nut. The cylinder head was also in iron and held down by seven bolts. The plug was centred above the exhaust valve and a blanked hole provided above the piston to enable its movement to be gauged while setting the timing.

The iron barrel of the ohv engines was also held down on four studs and a further four bolts held the cylinder head in place on a spigot. The head was also in iron and extended out on the right over the push rod tubes which clamped between it and the top of the crankcase. Valve wells were cast into the top of the head into which the guides were pressed and duplex valve springs were fitted for these engines.

Separate light alloy rocker boxes were bolted down over the valves to enclose them and each contained a single rocker which had a hardened adjustor screw with locknut at its outer end bearing on the valve cap. A valve lifter was fitted to the exhaust rocker box and both had an access cap for valve adjustment and a banjo oil connection to supply oil to the drilled rocker spindle.

The timing side could hardly have been simpler as it only comprised one pinion keyed to the end of the crankshaft with a gear above it on a live shaft carrying the two cams. Above the camshaft was located a fixed pin and on this pivoted two identical bellcranks, the inner one dealing with the inlet valve. The bellcranks had curved upper ends on the side valve engine to match the tappets, while for the ohv they had small cups to carry the push rods.

The timing gear was all carried in a circular chamber cast into the side of the crankcase and this was closed by a cover which was extended back and up for the magneto drive. This item, with a dynamo strapped to its back, was chain driven from a sprocket mounted on the end of the camshaft and both sprockets were threaded to take the same puller for dismantling. The camshaft had one further job to do and for this was machined with a pin at its extreme end off centre to the shaft axis so it moved in a circle. It was required to drive the twin plunger oil pump which was bolted to the cover and this contained suitable holes to pass the oil to and from

1946 twin port single with low level exhaust systems, telescopic forks and rigid frame

September 1947 *Motor Cycling* **advert aimed to show the wide spread of their exports and their priority**

the pump. Over the whole of the pump and magneto drive went an outer cover held by a series of screws, and on the cover went a legend of the model letters and, in 1945, the capacity as well. Later on only the letters were used and on occasion they were left blank.

The crankshaft was supported in the crank-case by a total of three races, two on the drive side and one on the timing. The touring models and the NH used ball races in all three places but the 500 cc Red Hunter was fitted with a lipped roller race on the timing side and a non-lipped roller plus a ball race on the drive side.

The engines had the usual Ariel cam lobe shock absorber on the output shaft and drove to the dry clutch via a single strand chain. The gearbox was a four-speed, footchange Burman, a type CP for the 350 and a BA for the others.

The frame was the well used prewar type with duplex rails beneath the engine and gearbox and single tubes for down, seat and top positions. The girder forks, saddles and instrument panels emphasised the prewar lines as did the flare of the front mudguard on some models and the unsprung headlamp.

For all that, they were very tough machines and eminently suited to those postwar years

The 1949 de luxe VG500 still much as in 1945 aside from the forks

when transport that was reliable over the poor roads of the period was the prime essential. Despite the austere times the Hunters managed to enliven the scene with their red tank finish.

In the middle of 1946 the Ariel forks appeared and at first the only singles to have them fitted were the Red Hunters. This did not last for long and when the 1947 range was announced late in August it was telescopics for all plus the link type rear suspension as an option. At that time rear suspension was still viewed with some suspicion in sporting circles and many riders averred that a rigid model handled better, some also maintaining that girders, with their high lateral rigidity, were also to be preferred. Thus the limited number of spring frames tended to go to the Four as this was looked upon as a tourer and thus allowed to wallow round corners.

There was some justification for the rider's views as some of the early forms of both telescopics and rear suspension lacked real damping and rigidity. Often they would bounce and pitch over the rough roads of the times and a good girder fork on a rigid frame was undoubtedly superior to a weak telescopic and wayward plunger.

Which possibly accounted for the road tests carried out by *The Motor Cycle* and *Motor Cycling* early in September, both being of Red Hunters with rigid frames. Both models had the new telescopics and both had the twin port head with low level pipes. The 'Blue Un' drew the 500 model VH on which they covered over 600 miles in good order. Top speed came out around 85 mph with third gear good for 70, while fuel consumption at a steady 50 mph came out at 79 mpg. Handling was light and the steering precise while the comfort, aided by the saddle, was considered excellent.

Braking was good with the front hub revised to fit the new forks but the rear pedal was too high for comfort and the fitment of the second exhaust pipe on the left prevented it from being lowered. Starting was first kick and the engine noise low, but both factors depended to some extent on the rider's use of the ignition control and correct throttle setting.

Given that the Hunter behaved in the manner of its forebears, it carried on the tradition of the English single. This required massive flywheels, lowish compression ratio, good transmission shock absorber, limited maximum revs and soft cam timing. The result was a totally relaxed way of travel that ate up the miles with ease and

The 1949 Red Hunter NH350 with its subtle differences from the NG and the VH, this one with twin port head

The VB600 for 1952 with painted tank, alloy head and tubular silencer

A 1951 Red Hunter under investigation, its tank has lost its paint but retains the chrome

ignored gradients which it rolled up without effort.

The 350 cc model NH which the 'Green Un' tested fitted this mould just as well as the larger model but was slower at 73 mph. The fuel consumption was similar as the machine was called on to cruise just as quickly and equally long journeys were undertaken without cramp or discomfort intervening. The handling was good enough to leave scars on the footrests and silencers on both sides and the brakes worked well, wet or dry. As on the 500, the speedometer was driven from the gearbox by an armoured cable that rose up past the oil tank like an uncoiling serpent.

The postwar Red Hunters carried on the traditions of the Ariel single very well and they were

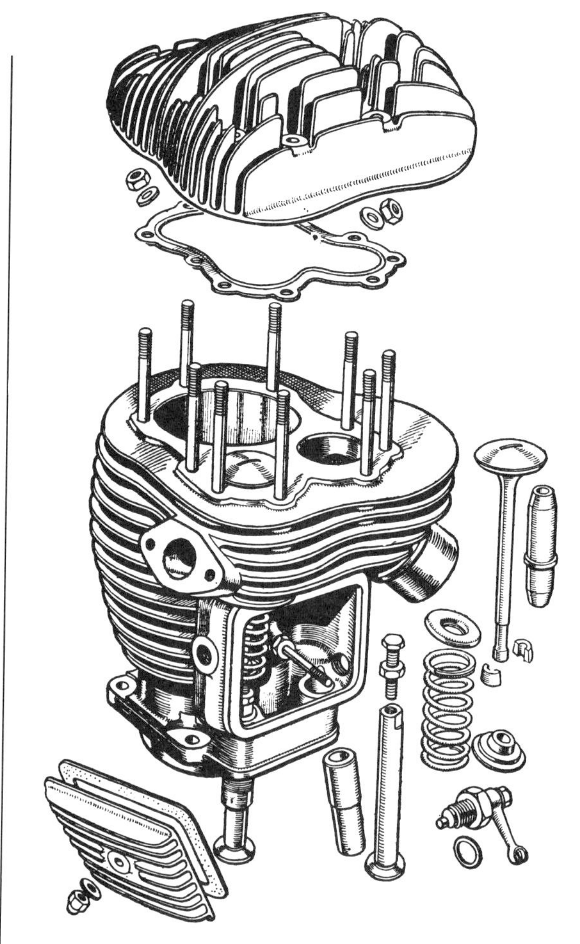

Details of the top half of the side valve engine with the alloy head as from 1952

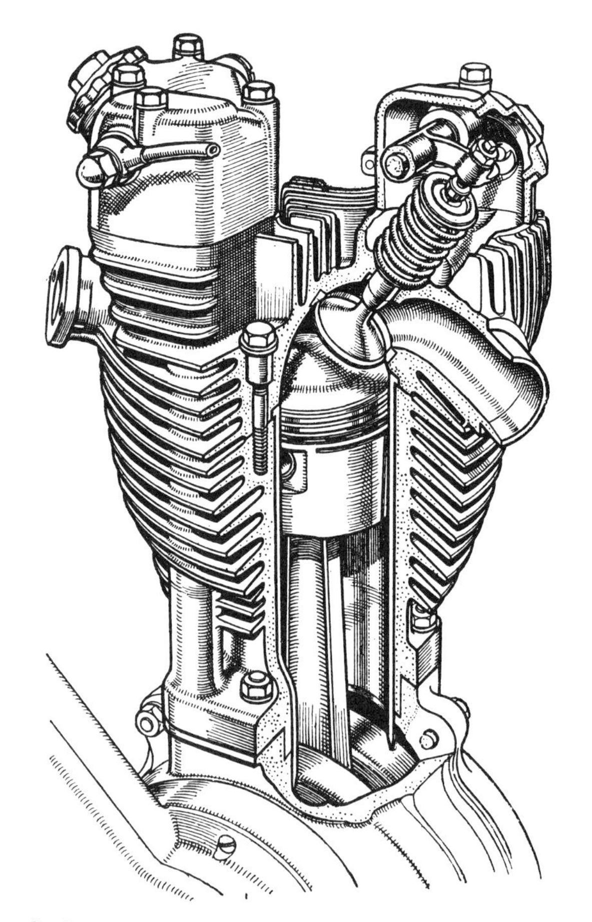

All-alloy single engine top half with integral pushrod tubes, five stud crankcase and head held by five sleeve nuts

a popular make among sportsmen and often pressed into use on scrambles course or grass track. At the other end of the scale the side valve VB plodded on its way, often hauling a sidecar along as in *The Motor Cycle* test late in 1947 when it had a Watsonian Monarch tourer bolted to it.

In this form it proved to be good for 61 mph with comfortable cruising at 45 mph. For the times this was more than acceptable, for most small saloon cars kept to a steady 30–40 mph and 60 mph on most roads was fast. The tested outfit performed well in most aspects but in braking illustrated the problems of adding weight without a sidecar stopper, as the figures certainly deterred the driver from following anything closely.

Completing the singles line-up were the two sizes of touring models from which the Hunters were derived and these formed the backbone of motorcycling in those austere postwar days, for they took men to work reliably and at the weekends, petrol ration permitting, allowed the owner to get himself and partner out into the country for a while.

So for 1948 there were no real changes and

Drive side of the all-alloy 500 cc single, the VHA, with cycle parts common to the range

they just carried on building bikes. The speedometers became the chronometric type and, by this time, the compression ratios had risen a little to 6·2:1 for the two 350s and 6·8:1 for the 500s.

During the spring of 1948 the experimental all-alloy single was seen ridden by Bob Ray in the Travers Trophy trial. The engine was a 500 and had a barrel that incorporated the push rod tubes and was held down by six studs with a further five retaining the head. The crankcase was in magnesium alloy and only these competition engines had the six stud base fixing.

There was no mention of this model in the 1949 range which had the common changes to forks and dynamo, a prop stand as standard, air filter option and a neater rear number plate. The option of a two port head and upswept or normal exhaust pipes continued for the 350 single but not for the 500. This standardised on a single downswept pipe and all exhausts gained finned pipe clips. As on the other models, the seal holder at the top of the moving fork leg was chrome plated.

It was August 1949 before more was heard of the alloy engine and then it was announced as the power unit of a new competition Hunter model VCH available to trials or scrambles specification. In either form it came ready for action with a racing BTH magneto, low exhaust pipe with upswept silencer, no lights and alloy mudguards.

The engine was based on that seen earlier and had much in common with the iron Red Hunter including the 6·8:1 compression ratio. For those able to obtain a more amenable fuel, an alternative piston giving a ratio of 7·5:1 was also available. The cylinder barrel had an iron liner pressed into it and the head was cast around a spectacle frame of the two valve seats and the plug boss. The push rod tunnels were cast as two separate holes in the barrel and five studs were screwed into the top face to take the sleeve nuts which held the head.

Lubrication was as on the singles with the small, 350 cc model, oil tank fitted and breather pipes from the crankcase mouth on the drive side and the back of the magneto drive case as usual. The rocker feed pipe was positioned more out of the way to the rear of the cylinder.

The primary drive was normal Ariel with a two-plate clutch and wide ratio gearbox being offered for trials use and a three-plate plus close gears

Timing side of VHA, in this case in a rigid frame, a model dropped late in 1953 after a short existence

VHA in centre of model line-up in Johnson Motors Inc. showrooms, the Ariel West Coast distributors in California

for scrambles. The frame was special with short wheelbase and high ground clearance, but was constructed on the same lines as the others. It was fitted with the usual telescopics with stronger springs, while the hubs were stock. Tyres were Dunlop Universal for trials and Sports for scrambles, and mudguards were polished light alloy with flat and tubular stays. A rear stand was fitted, a toolbox occupied the position normally taken by the battery and the rider's comfort was looked after by a saddle.

The VCH was in the range list for 1950 as a rigid model only. All the other singles had the option of the spring frame and also the newly

Right **Brochure for the competition model VCH with all alloy engine and available for trials or scrambles use**

The ARIEL Competition HUNTER

500 c.c. MODEL V.C.H.

This model has been specially designed for trials and competition work in which light weight and ease of handling over the most arduous courses are the prime considerations.

Although light in weight, this machine retains the robust construction characteristic of all Ariel products, while the engine has ample power with positive control at all speeds.

TECHNICAL DATA

Wheelbase	54″	
Overall length	84″	
Handlebar width... ...	27″	
Saddle height	30″	
Ground clearance ...	5½″	
Weight, dry	300 lb.	
Fuel consumption ...	50/60 m.p.g.	
Oil consumption ...	2,000 m.p.g.	
Engine b.h.p. at	25	
Engine r.p.m.	6,000	
	Wide	Close
Solo gear ratio, top	6.05	5.75
Solo gear ratio, third	9.16	7.2
Solo gear ratio, second	12.6	9.7
Solo gear ratio, low	19.1	15.3
Engine sprocket solo ...	19 teeth	
Compression ratio ...	6.8	
Links in front chain ...	80 × ½″ pitch	
Links in rear chain ...	91 × ⅝″ pitch	

SPECIFICATION

Engine: 81.8 × 95 mm. (497 c.c.) O.H.V. single cylinder. Aluminium alloy cylinder barrel with nickel iron liner. Aluminium alloy cylinder head with stainless steel valve inserts, highly polished ports, forged steel flywheels, large diameter mainshafts mounted on two heavy-duty roller bearings and one ball bearing. Large double roller caged big end bearing. The engine is specially bench tested and tuned.

Lubrication: Dry sump, employing dual plunger pumps—large capacity supply pump—half gallon capacity separate oil tank.

Ignition: Magneto B.T.H. racing type.

Gearbox: Four speed wide ratio, foot control, two-plate neoprene clutch, built-in speedometer drive. (Close ratio gears and three-plate neoprene clutch for scramble machines).

Speedometer: 120 m.p.h. trip mounted on front forks.

Frame: Short wheelbase, fully brazed steel tube construction. Polished duralumin mudguards, flat and tubular stays. Tool box.

Transmission: Polished aluminium oilbath primary chaincase, rear chain fully protected.

Exhaust System: Single-port low-level exhaust pipe with upswept silencer.

Wheels: Dunlop Trials Universal tyres 4.00 × 19″ rear, 3.00 × 21″ front. (Sports tyres to special order). Chromium rims, red centres, lined gold.

Fuel Tank: 2½ gallon capacity, finished chromium and red, lined gold.

SPRING FRAME CANNOT BE FITTED TO THIS MODEL

PRICE
including Speedometer
£180 . 0 . 0
plus Purchase Tax
£48 . 12 . 0

ARIEL MOTORS LIMITED · BIRMINGHAM · ENGLAND

A 1953 NH350 Red Hunter during a road test. Fitted with link rear suspension and dualseat but no pillion rests

Advert for 600 cc model VB shown in the optional frame with rear suspension

ENGINE: Specially designed for solo or heavy duty sidecar work. 86.4 × 102 mm. 598 c.c. (3.4 × 4.01 = 36.5 cubic inches). Cast iron cylinder barrel with polished aluminium alloy cylinder head. Heavy duty ball bearings on both sides of mainshaft. Totally enclosed valve gear. Double row roller connecting rod big end bearing. Amal carburetter. Dual plunger oil pump. Lucas manual ignition control.

FRAME: Full cradle type, rigid, with lugs for sidecar attachment either side. (Ariel patented plunger rear suspension at extra.) Forged steel girder spring-up rear and strong tubular front stands.

MUDGUARDS: Wide D section with tubular stays. Rear guard can be lifted for easy wheel removal.

BRAKES: Ariel design of great power, ensuring positive and progressive action. 7 inch diameter front and rear. Car type fulcrum adjustment.

LIGHTING EQUIPMENT: 7½ inch headlamp incorporating lighting switch and ammeter. 56 watt voltage controlled magdyno. 6 volt battery. Stop and tail lamp. Electric horn.

FINISH: Superbly finished throughout in best quality black enamel.

introduced quickly detachable rear wheel. Most of the other changes were as on the twins with the saddle height raised an inch, tubular mudguard stays, modified rear brake pedal and the options of air cleaner and ribbed front tyre. The new type of Lucas headlamp was fitted and on the singles the light switch was mounted in the rear of the shell.

The standard finishes remained unaltered with the VCH copying the Red Hunter, aside from its alloy mudguards. In addition a green and chrome option was offered for the de-luxe models and the VB with this colour applied to tank and wheel rim centres.

Early in the year *Motor Cycling* reported on a 500 cc Red Hunter fitted with the spring frame and a ribbed front tyre. It proved to be good for 86 mph and accelerated briskly to the 70 plus cruising speed used for much of the test. The brakes worked well and the machine was comfortable to ride. Criticisms concerned piston slap, a gearbox that was audible if rushed, and the tank top speedometer that was anything but quick and easy to read. For all that, it continued the Red Hunter tradition of offering sporting and reliable performance.

The speedometer problem was overcome for 1951 when the singles adopted the diecast top fork crown carrying the instrument. The two de-luxe models did not continue as they were less popular and production needs made it sensible to rationalise on fewer models. Most of the changes again copied the twins so the mudguard and its stays, the lifting handle, battery clamp, front number plate, barrel-shaped saddle springs, and switch with ammeter on a panel in the rear of the handlamp shell, all faithfully reflected these models.

As on them, the panel in the tank went and in the case of the singles the oil gauge was also dispensed with. Thanks to this the tank capacity increased by a couple of pints in each case.

The one change that was special to the singles that year was to the cams and followers. In place of the early arrangement came one designed to reduce wear on both components. This was done by changing from two overlapping cams to a single one of twice the width. This allowed the follower pad to also double in length and the arrangement was easy to devise by moving the cam form on the shaft and the follower pad to suit.

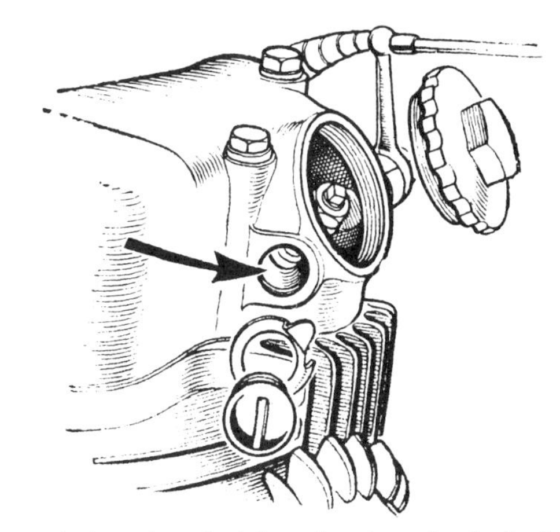

Access hole and cap lock introduced on ohv singles from 1955

The followers were no longer identical as the inlet was of conventional form, while the exhaust had a forked pivot which fitted either side of the inlet. Despite this the new design was cheaper to produce than the old and the wear was much reduced. In addition to doubling the area subject to load the opportunity was also taken to modify the cam profile to include quietening ramps on both opening and closing sides.

As on the other models, the singles had to alter their tank finish early in 1951 due to the nickel shortage and thus these became all painted, lined and fitted with a new badge.

Another test was carried out on the VH in the middle of the year, this time by *The Motor Cycle* and in both solo and sidecar forms. Speeds were 85 and 63 mph in the two guises and the model continued to uphold the Hunter traditions.

1952 brought more changes and a new model, the all-alloy road single typed VHA. This had a

top half on the lines of the VCH with the five stud Hunter crankcase. It thus had the integral push rod tunnels in the barrel but otherwise was little different from the standard Red Hunter. All the singles were fitted with the Burman GB gearbox during 1952 and the ohv models received split skirt pistons to reduce their noise. Head gaskets were also added.

Other general changes were to the oil tank, except for the NH, the adoption of deeper fins and a more forward siting of the prop stand. The side valve model was fitted with a light alloy cylinder head which raised the compression ratio and the power. The head was retained by a total of nine studs, two more than before, and with the deeper fins the barrel was a new casting.

The 1954 scrambles model HS with all alloy engine, swinging fork frame, hefty dualseat and open pipe

It also finally lost its styled silencer and was fitted with a tubular one.

The competition Hunter had the added fin area as on the other models and also had the frame fork ends altered to raise the ground clearance. The mudguard section was changed to increase the clearance to the tyres and thus be more suited to scrambles use.

During the year *Motor Cycling* tested the new all-alloy Hunter and also the side valve machine with a sidecar attached. The VHA proved to be good for 88·2 mph and was cruised at 75 for long periods. The new type of gearbox functioned well but the gap between the two upper ratios was greater than it had been and was thought excessive. In other respects it was the same breed of animal from the same stable as before.

In contrast, the VB with its new alloy head was a horse of very different type, built for solid collar work. It pulled the single seat Watsonian along at up to 53 mph with a normal cruising rate of 45, a traditional sidecar speed. In the main it performed as expected but did stop a couple of times due to water in the ignition. This demonstrated very effectively that access to the points was limited when a sidecar was fitted and that the high tension pick-up and lead were well tucked away just behind the cylinder.

As a complete change *The Motor Cycle* had a competition Hunter out in the hills and reported well on it. The model they tested was fitted with an optional, bolt-through, light alloy tank and this saved about 6 lbs of weight. With the ignition retarded the engine would pull from zero revs and accelerate away cleanly when required. The exhaust pipe continued to run under the timing cover and gearbox before kinking up to the silencer which was tilted up. No air filter was fitted but a wire gauze clipped to the carburettor helped to keep dirt at bay and only a rear stand was supplied.

The 350 cc Red Hunter gained the larger oil tank in 1953 and, like the other ohv models, had the rocker box oil feed taken from the return pipe near the tank. As on the twins, the rear brake was cable operated when the spring frame was specified, a new prop stand was fitted except on the VB, and the Diacon rear lamp was used other than on the NH and VB which had a smaller design. A dualseat became an option for the ohv models and a dynamo and lighting kit was offered as an option for the competition VCH. More variety of colours appeared with the alloy Hunter in Wedgewood blue and white lining, with the option of claret red and gold lining as used for the iron VH Hunter. Most models were listed as being available in any of the finishes used for the singles range, and all road models were fitted with the unloved, underslung pilot lamp.

Factory picture of the 1954–55 model HS all clean and tidy as delivered complete with centre stand

Motor Cycling road tested the smaller Red Hunter during the spring and their model was fitted with the spring frame and an optional piston giving a compression ratio of 7·4:1. This was sufficient to push it along at 74 mph with a comfortable cruising speed just under 60. For the rest, it was a typical Ariel with good brakes, adequate handling with a little pitching on occasion, and reasonable quietness although the piston could still be heard when cold.

In February, Clive Bennett of the Ariel experimental department was seen at the Colmore Trial with a competition Hunter fitted with the Earles forks. When the road models were listed they included an alloy Hunter equipped with the forks and this model was called the VHA Mk II and given the name Hunt Marshall. This exercise came to nothing but in scrambles three machines began to appear with Earles forks and a new all-welded duplex frame with swinging fork rear suspension.

This was the frame design that was adopted by most of the range for 1954 and when this was announced it was seen that there were quite a number of changes for both road and competition models. On the road the all-alloy Red Hunter VHA was dropped and the VH modified to use the alloy head on an iron barrel cast in the mould of the alloy one with integral push rod tunnels. The methods of fixing both head and barrel remained the same with each fitting on to five studs and retained by nuts or sleeve nuts. The 350 continued with its all iron engine and separate push rod tubes but was fitted with a four gallon tank, as were the VB and the VH.

The tank aside, the side valve 600 continued unchanged in its rigid frame fitted with a saddle but the two Hunters went into the new swinging fork frame. With that went a new oil tank, toolbox, horn position, dualseat and air filter as on the twins. All three singles had the new style of tank with chrome plated flutes and the Hunter

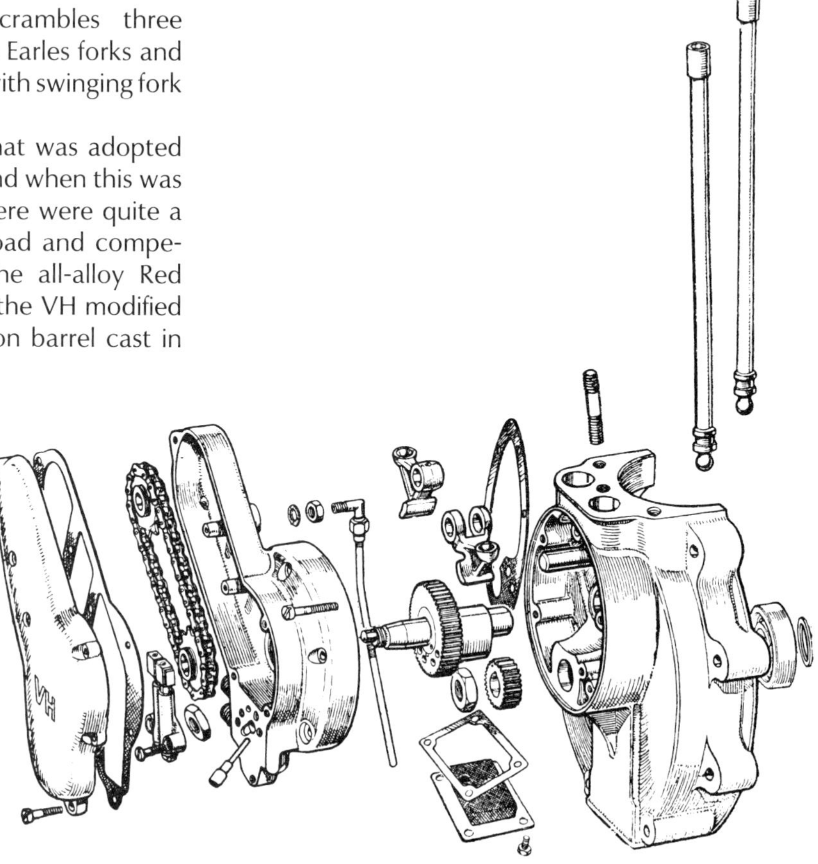

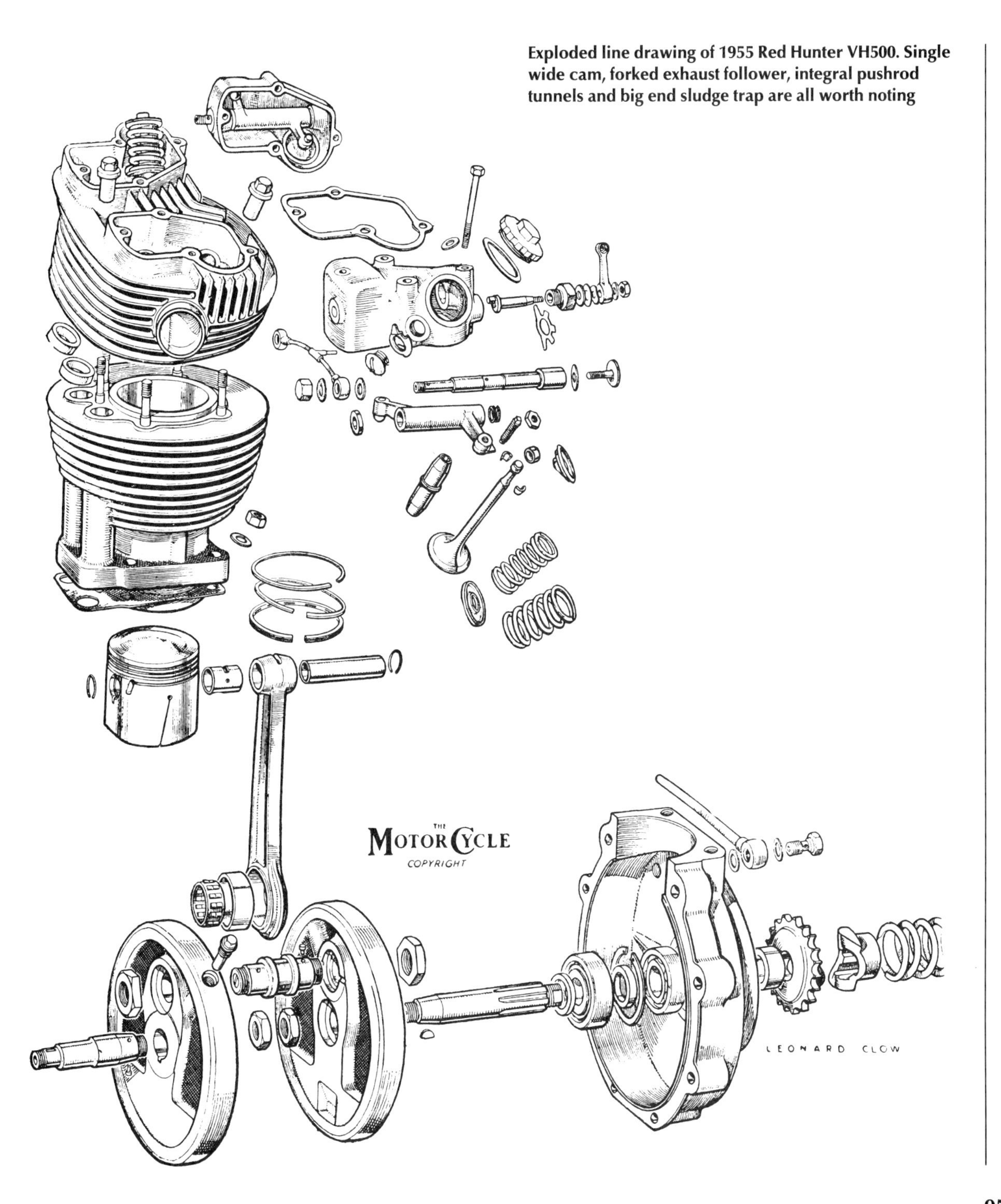

Exploded line drawing of 1955 Red Hunter VH500. Single wide cam, forked exhaust follower, integral pushrod tunnels and big end sludge trap are all worth noting

ones copied the twins with the deep chrome band on each side, and round plastic tank badges. The VB tank did not have this band and was fitted with a thin linear badge.

In place of the dual purpose VCH came two models, both of 500 cc, with the HS designed for scrambles use and the HT for trials. Both used the all-alloy engine with the Hunter-type bottom half and the HS ran on a compression ratio of 9·1:1 and produced 33 bhp at 6250 rpm. It drove a GB gearbox with the normal road ratios and a range of engine sprockets was available to suit the course the machine was to run on.

The HS used the swinging fork duplex frame and came complete with the normal centre stand. The oil tank was a smaller and slimmer version of the one used on the road models and the exhaust pipe curled above the timing case to an open exit at waist level. A dual seat was fitted and a racing Lucas magneto, while the option of the mag-dyno and a quickly detachable lighting set remained. Unlike the road engine, the scrambler had an oil seal fitted into the drive side crankcase half and this ran on the drive shaft to prevent oil leaking out into the chaincase. This small problem only arose because the competition engine ran at high speed all the time.

The scrambler was finished off with competition tyres, narrow chrome plated mudguards and a small petrol tank, all features also used for the trials HT model. The engine for this had a much lower 5·6:1 compression ratio and the same cam timing as the road models, unlike the HS which had much more overlap. A Lucas wader magneto was specified, again with the mag-dyno and lighting option, and a standard type 6 Amal carburettor in place of the TT one used on the HS.

The HT had a wide ratio Burman gearbox and the mechanics went into a short wheelbase rigid frame with single down tube. The usual telescopic front forks were fitted and similar wheels to the HS but with Universal tyres. The oil tank was the 4 pint one from the road range and the exhaust followed the same line as on the VCH but with a smooth bend up to the silencer in place of the earlier kink. A saddle was provided for the rider and a speedometer mounted on the top yoke. For both HS and HT models a light alloy petrol tank and mudguards were optional.

The VB600 in 1955 in swinging fork frame with all the details common to the other singles for that year

A *Motor Cycling* road test of an NH showed it to be just as quick as ever at 75 mph but with improved comfort and handling, thanks to the new frame. In other respects it was as before which was to be expected for the basic motorcycle had changed little in its essentials over its long lifespan. One area that had declined was the silencing, for the exhaust note was considered too noisy.

1955 brought a number of detail changes except for the side valve model, which became available in the swinging fork frame with all the cycle parts as used by the Hunters. The rigid frame version continued to be offered to the diehards who would accept nothing else for sidecar use. The detail changes again copied the twins with chrome top rings in the engine, Monobloc carburettors, a steering lock, extended rear mudguard, screw-in horn button, oil tank filler cap more tucked in, longer rear brake pedal and 19 in. front wheels.

On the ohv engines went flexible oil pipes and inspection caps in the sides of the rocker boxes to make valve clearance checking easier. These caps held down shaped washers which locked into the serrated edge of the rocker box cap to prevent it from coming undone. On the 500 cc engine alone the exhaust valve size was reduced and the two competition models were unchanged.

The Motor Cycle road tested the new style model VB with a child/adult saloon sidecar attached and in this form it proved to be good for 55 mph with strong pulling power. Heavily laden it would plod on at around 45 often maintaining this gait up main road hills, albeit with a rather loud exhaust note when on a wide throttle. As had happened before, rain was inclined to drip into the magneto points housing.

In the middle of the year the prototype full-width light alloy front hub was seen on the Ariel twins run in the ISDT selection tests and when the 1956 range was announced all the singles were fitted with this and a matching one at the back. As on the twins, the lubrication arrangements for the rear chain were changed, an optional rear chaincase offered, the rather complex rod and cable operation for the rear brake fitted, the headlight cowl added, the pilot light fitted into the main reflector, a straight pull twistgrip

1956 model HS with oil tank on left and massive air cleaner on right. Full width hubs front and rear

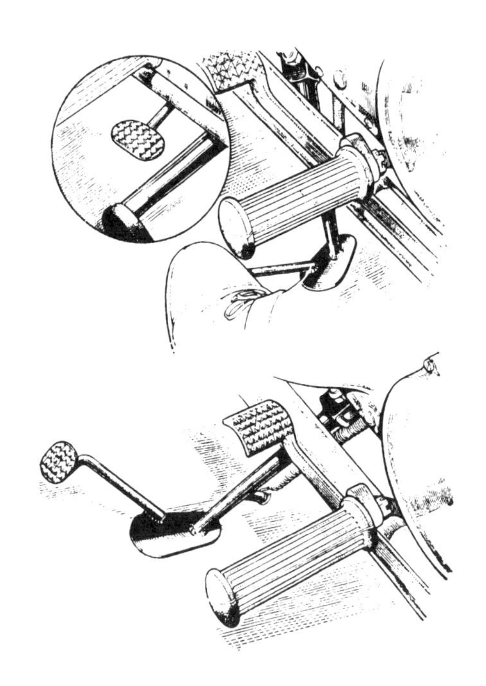

Left **Prop stand with extension pedal for rider convenience adopted in 1957**

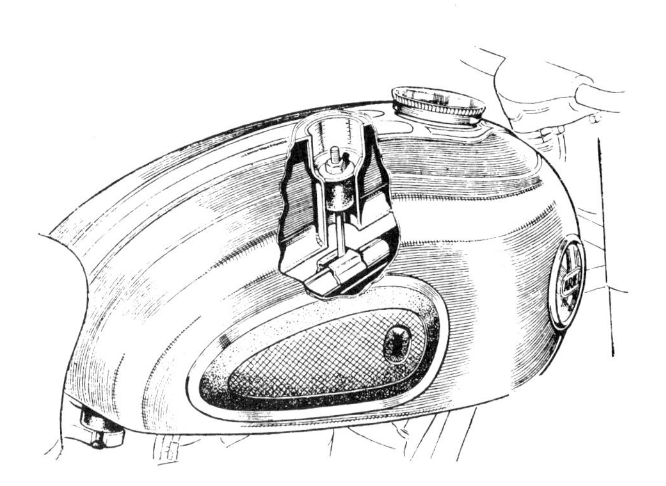

Below **Centre bolt tank fixing used from 1957 on twins and singles, covered by tank strap**

employed, and the handlebars cleaned up with an alloy clamp and combined horn button and dipswitch.

Changes only applicable to the singles affected the NH, VB, HT and HS. The 350 Hunter was given a light alloy cylinder head and an iron barrel with integral push rod tunnels, so copied the larger VH. Its compression ratio was also raised to 7·5 : 1. The change for the VB was the dropping of the rigid model, while the HT was given a new diamond frame with swinging fork rear suspension which retained the short wheelbase of the rigid model. With the new frame went a slightly smaller fuel tank. It was the basis for what was to become the best known trials machine of all time. The HS had its oil tank moved to the left to give room for a large air cleaner connected by hose to the carburettor.

In May the new trials model, now called the HT5, met up with the man destined to make it and himself famous—Sammy Miller, who was to earn the soubriquet of the worlds greatest trials rider. The basis of this was achieved using the Ariel, although when he first rode the 500 Miller was already very successful in trials using a succession of two-strokes, and also in road racing at works level. He was due to ride a James in the Scottish but a chance series of events led him to the Ariel and so, for 6 days, he rode GOV 132—a registration number that was to become well known. He took home an award and must have had his problems for a photo in *The Motor Cycle* shows him minus his front mudguard. At that time the HT was a standard model but over the years it was to be improved.

In March 1956 came the separate flutes for the road model singles and more tests of the Red Hunters merely emphasized that the more it changed the more it remained as the early 1930s machine with its sporting but controllable performance.

The flutes disappeared when the 1957 range was announced, as the singles were fitted with the same single bolt tank as the twins. The capa-

The Mark III model HS of 1957 built as a trail machine rather than a scrambler

Late type VH as built from 1957–59 with valanced mudguard, full width hubs and cowled headlamp

city was up a little and the holding bolt was hidden by a top chrome band. Virtually all the changes mirrored the twins with the added clutch inserts, cross strap for the headlight cowl, deeply valanced front mudguard without forward stay and with the front number plate on the side valances, prop stand pedal added and the smaller kneegrips on an alloy surround.

New was a 350 cc version of the trials model typed the HT3. This was a repeat of the 500 aside from gearing and the engine, which used the NH dimensions in an all-alloy unit of less overall height. Both models changed to 2·75 in. section front tyres but otherwise the competition machines, including the HS, continued as they were.

During 1957 Miller rode the Ariel extensively as a member of the work team and at the end of the year joined the company to work in the competition department. He began a weight-reducing exercise on his machine uncertain as to how much he would be allowed to change from the stock HT5. Not a great deal at that point as it turned out but this did not stop him from having a very successful season.

There were no changes to the road or competition singles for 1958 for they were coming to the end of their lives as the company changed its policy and direction away from four-strokes. The first victim of this decision was the long serving side valve VB which was not listed for 1959, while the other models continued as they were.

350 cc version, the NH, virtually a replica of the VH aside from the mark on the timing cover

Next to go were the competition machines early in the year which just left the two Hunters.

While the singles range contracted Sammy Miller went from success to success on his Ariel with innumerable wins in the major trials events. At the end of 1959 the four-stroke range came to an end and with it the Ariel works trials team. The competition shop was shut and Miller was transferred to the development department. Fortunately he was allowed to buy GOV 132 for a nominal pound and allowed one day a week to work on the machine, but as a trials rider reverted to the status of a private entrant.

So there were no more four-stroke singles, but the Miller legend really began to take off and with the restriction to keep to standard parts gone, the weight of GOV 132 began to come down. Rims became light alloy, at a time when the trials world swore by steel, and the hubs were Ariel Leader.

This sufficed for a while, but late in 1960 a revised machine appeared with a new frame built using Reynolds 531 tubing. The pattern remained a diamond with single top, down and saddle tubes and a light sub-frame supported the tops of the rear units which controlled the rear fork. The left arm of the fork acted as a reservoir for the chain oil. The seat tube doubled as an oil tank with a filter at the top and the front forks

Changing the plug in a late single outside a dealer selling a 1950 Ariel for £35 and another for £30

The 1958 trials HT5, this one all polished up and on show

remained Ariel but with an alloy top crown.

Everything was well tucked in and lightened extensively with the seat pan, primary chaincase, magneto shield and number plates all in fibreglass. Another phenomenal season followed and then another, to the annoyance of the parent BSA company which had its own team of riders. That firm were hardly overjoyed at the continuous run of success by a rider who used a machine built by a subsidiary and one that was also not in production, even as a road model.

By 1962 the Miller Ariel had a one-piece moulding forming the seat base and the rear mudguard, and titanium parts were beginning to appear to cut the weight even further. One of the less usual features was the exit hole from the silencer which was arranged to blow the mud off the rear tyre. The front forks had become Manx Norton and the front mudguard was in fibreglass. That year Miller won the Scottish 6-Days and a good many other events and the weight of the Ariel was down to 245 lb.

It remained around that point from then on while Miller continued to dominate the trials scene, despite little support from the BSA group. It was revised a little in 1964 and an experiment carried out using leading link forks, but this was not taken any further.

By this time Miller knew that it was only his ability that was keeping the lighter two-strokes at bay. They were steadily making it harder for him to win and, with little help or interest from

Line drawing, partly cut-away, of the 1958 HT5 with light subframe, the HT3 was similar, Miller's machine much lighter

the factory, he decided a change was necessary. So when his contract expired he ignored factory suggestions that he should sign for BSA and went foreign to Bultaco.

His departure was on a high note for he had won the Scottish once again and the last event before he changed machines was the British Experts which he won for the third time on the famous Ariel single. The machine, and another he also used, went on sale but in later years he bought GOV 132 back, restored it and presented it to Beaulieu where it now stands.

5 Colt, Pixie and the pantomime horse

The Colt had been the name used in prewar times for a pair of sporting, high-kicking, 250s, and was revived postwar for a lightweight designed to plug the gap at the lower end of the Ariel range. It was part of the 1954 line-up so came along at a time when a number of firms were adding such machines to their lists to cajole customers to their marque, hopefully for all time.

Like the 650 twin announced at the same time, the new Colt (given the type letters LH) owed much to the group technology and had many features common to the BSA Bantam, C10 and C11. Unlike them it was a 200 so was in direct competition to the new Triumph Cub which grew up from the Terrier that year.

The Colt was a straightforward machine built for the commuter and learner market with a single cylinder, overhead valve engine, four-speed gearbox and with plunger rear suspension. The engine was based on dimensions of 60 × 70 mm which gave an actual capacity of 198 cc and developed 10 bhp at 5600 rpm on a compression ratio of 7·5 : 1.

The engine construction was a dead ringer for the BSA C11G of 250 cc and followed conventional English practice for the period. The crankcase was cast in aluminium and split vertically on the centre line with a small sump plate fixed to the underside by four bolts. It supported the built up crankshaft in a ball race on the drive side and a phosphor bronze bush on the timing one. The big end had a single row of uncaged

Pre-production 200 Colt fitted with flat Bantam silencer and with other details that were altered

rollers which ran direct on the crankpin and this was pulled up to the wheels by nuts. The connecting rod was a steel forging which ran on the big end rollers but was bushed at the small end.

The piston was in aluminium with a split skirt and the usual single scraper and two compression rings. Its gudgeon pin was retained by circlips and it ran in an iron barrel held down onto six studs. The barrel had a cast-in tunnel on the right for the two push rods and this was extended up into the light alloy cylinder head so the valve gear was totally enclosed.

The head had austenitic iron valve seats cast into place and was held to the barrel by seven studs screwed into its lower surface. A head gasket was fitted and the nuts for the head studs fitted between the barrel fins as on the Ariel 500 twin. Each valve was held to its seat by duplex springs retained by a collar and split collets and the two assemblies sat in a single well. To the top surface of the head was bolted a rocker support forging and this had pins machined at each

1955 Colt with clean ohv engine, separate gearbox, plunger frame and substantial teles

The Colt from the left showing typical BSA pressed steel chaincase and Bantam rear wheel

Factory clean Colt of 1956 with separate switches but still with straight inlet tract

end at an angle. The rockers lay across the head and, thanks to the angle of their support pins, were in line with the valves. They were held in place by split-pinned nuts with spring washers to take up the end float and had adjustors on the push rod side of the usual screw and locknut type. A light alloy cover went over the top of the rocker assembly to enclose the entire mechanism.

The timing side was very simple and much as on the larger singles with a pinion on the crankshaft meshed with a gear above it on the camshaft. Above this went a fixed pin and on that pivoted two bellcrank cam followers, one for each valve. These were laid out so that the outer cam had the follower positioned ahead of the camshaft centre line and was for the inlet valve. The push rod lay back at an angle and was thus in line with the valve itself when viewed from the side. The exhaust side was similar with the push rod tilted forward so the two rods crossed over. Incorrect assembly was impossible as the crankcase top had two holes drilled for the push rods so they could only be placed in the correct manner.

The camshaft ran in bushes, one in the crankcase and the other in the timing case, which also supported the outer end of the cam follower pin. The end of the camshaft was taper bored and to this was attached the ignition centrifugal advance mechanism and the points cam with a pin

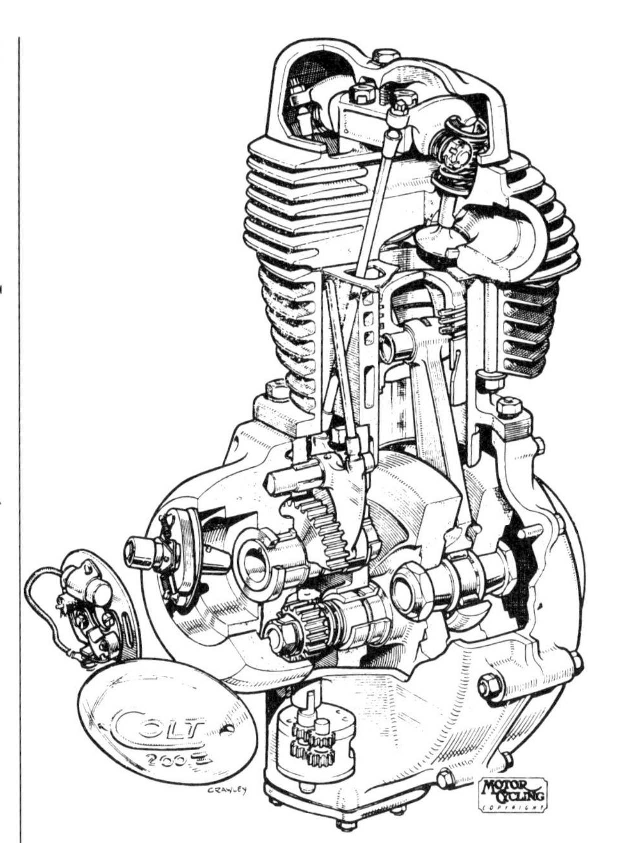

The simple Colt engine with its crossed pushrods, the design a copy of the C11G

to key the parts together at the correct position. The timing case carried the points and condenser on a backplate which could be rotated for fine adjustment of the timing and this was concealed by a cover bearing the legend 'Colt 200'.

Lubrication was dry sump from a separate oil tank and the supply and return pipes were the only external connections. The pump was a double gear type which fitted in the underside of the timing side crankcase and was driven by a worm machined with the timing pinion and inboard of it. A vertical shaft took the drive down to the pump and access to this was via the sump plate. The oil was supplied to the pump via a filter in the tank and forced under pressure past a valve to the main bearing bush. This was drilled to supply the mainshaft and this connected to the crankpin via drill-ways. The remainder of the engine relied on oil mist for lubrication and the oil finally drained back to the sump. There it was collected by the scavenge pump and returned to the oil tank, and the pump was protected by a gauze filter and a ball valve in the pick-up pipe.

The engine was supplied with mixture by a type 6 Amal carburettor and separate float chamber, while the exhaust side was by a low level pipe which was a push fit into the cylinder head. The silencer shown on the initial release was the early BSA Bantam type as used on the first D1, and known as the flat type due to its form. This was not fitted to the production Colt which had a tubular silencer.

Transmission was by chain in a pressed steel case to a new Burman four-speed gearbox. This was a lightweight unit designed for the up-to-250 cc machines but followed English convention in most features. Thus the sleeve gear was concentric with the mainshaft with the layshaft underneath and both clutch and final drive went on the left. The clutch had three plain plates and two lined with cork so ran happily in the oil in the chaincase. The clutch centre incorporated a shock absorber and the centre of the pressure plate carried a hardened screw adjustor.

On the right the clutch lift mechanism was a multi-start thread with hardened central thrust pin and a flat strip lever twisted to give it rigidity and to suit the clutch cable end. The thread housing was circular with a single lobe and this could be located in the end cover in a choice of positions to give the best lever action before it was retained by a circlip.

The gears were carried in a shell with a deep end cover on the right and were selected by twin forks mounted on rods at the back of the box. They were moved by a flat camplate and this was directly turned by the positive stop mechanism moved by the gear pedal. The camplate was pivoted on a pin screwed into the rear face of

The Colt as built from 1957–59. Note the odd curved inlet tract which mounts the air filter out to the right

the gearbox shell and restrained by a spring-loaded arm which dropped into detents as the plate rotated. On the prototype the arm was extended and moved a gear indicator rod which was dispensed with in production.

The mainshaft ran in ball races, while the layshaft went into bushes and the main shell carried the mounting lugs for the assembly. The end cover supported the gearchange mechanism and the pawl and ratchet kickstarter which worked on bottom gear on the layshaft. An outer cover concealed all these parts, supported the outer ends of the two pedal spindles, and was fitted with a large cap which gave access to the clutch cable and a means of filling the box with oil.

The engine and gearbox were mounted in an all-welded open diamond frame with plunger rear suspension. It was pure BSA C10L down to the mounting points for that model's saddle springs but at the front went better quality forks with hydraulic damping. They were very typical of the group and most likely came from the C11.

The brake sizes were those of the C10L at 5·5 in. front and 5 in. rear but unlike that model, which shared its hubs with the 150 cc Bantam, the Colt used the more substantial construction of knock-out spindle at the front. At the rear it stuck to the Bantam hub with the same sprocket which accounted for the odd feature of the final chain being narrower than the primary.

The wheel rims were WM1 section and for the

A Colt well modified for trials riding with swinging fork rear end. Used in 1957 Scottish by Clive Bell who retired

announcement carried 3·00 × 19 in. tyres, but these changed to 2·75 in. in production. The front mudguard and its stays came from the C11G but the rear was C10G but fitted with a boxed-in rear number plate. The front plate had the usual Ariel surround so was not bare.

As on the BSA the area between engine and gearbox was cowled in by a steel pressing and a toolbox fitted into the loop of the chainstays. The oil tank went on the right balanced by the battery on the left, and behind that went the horn. The electrics were coil ignition and an alternator fixed on the left side of the engine outboard of the primary drive sprocket. The rotor was keyed to the crankshaft and the stator fitted inside the chaincase and connected to a large rectifier mounted beneath the dualseat. An emergency start switch allowed all the generator output to be fed to the coil in the event of the battery being flat, and part of the control of the normal output was by a resistance wire in the harness.

The ignition and lighting switches were combined as one unit in the 6 in. headlamp shell and this was cowled to the forks by a pressing that formed the shrouds between the crowns and also supported the shell. On the top crown went an 80 mph speedometer on the prototype, but this became a 70 mph instrument in production.

The petrol tank copied the rest of the range with chrome plated flutes on the shoulders and

The Ariel Pixie with small ohv engine mounted in subframe from spine beam with trailing links at the front

round plastic badges. Kneegrips were fitted to the tank which was lined, and the initial finish was in black and chrome but in production this changed to deep Brunswick green with the dual-seat to match.

The success of the design was borne out by the lack of changes in the first months of production and the minimal alterations introduced for 1955. Chief among these was the move to the Amal Monobloc carburettor and this was fitted with a round air filter. Also in the engine a ramp cam form was adopted which retained the existing timing but eased the way the clearance was taken up, and the push rod diameter was increased a little to stiffen them up.

The method of adjusting the clutch was revised so that the pressure plate lost its central screw which was moved into the clutch worm on the right. A hardened pad went between screw and push rod and the housing only needed to fit into one position in the end cover so the result was an easier mechanism to use. The change also meant that adjustment did not require the chaincase to be opened up.

The other changes were to the tyres which went back up to the 3·00 in section, and the mudguards which were made deeper and wider to suit the tyres. The stays for the rear mudguard were changed for a single tube each side bent to run in to the top of the plunger housing and out to the guard again. The right side tube was

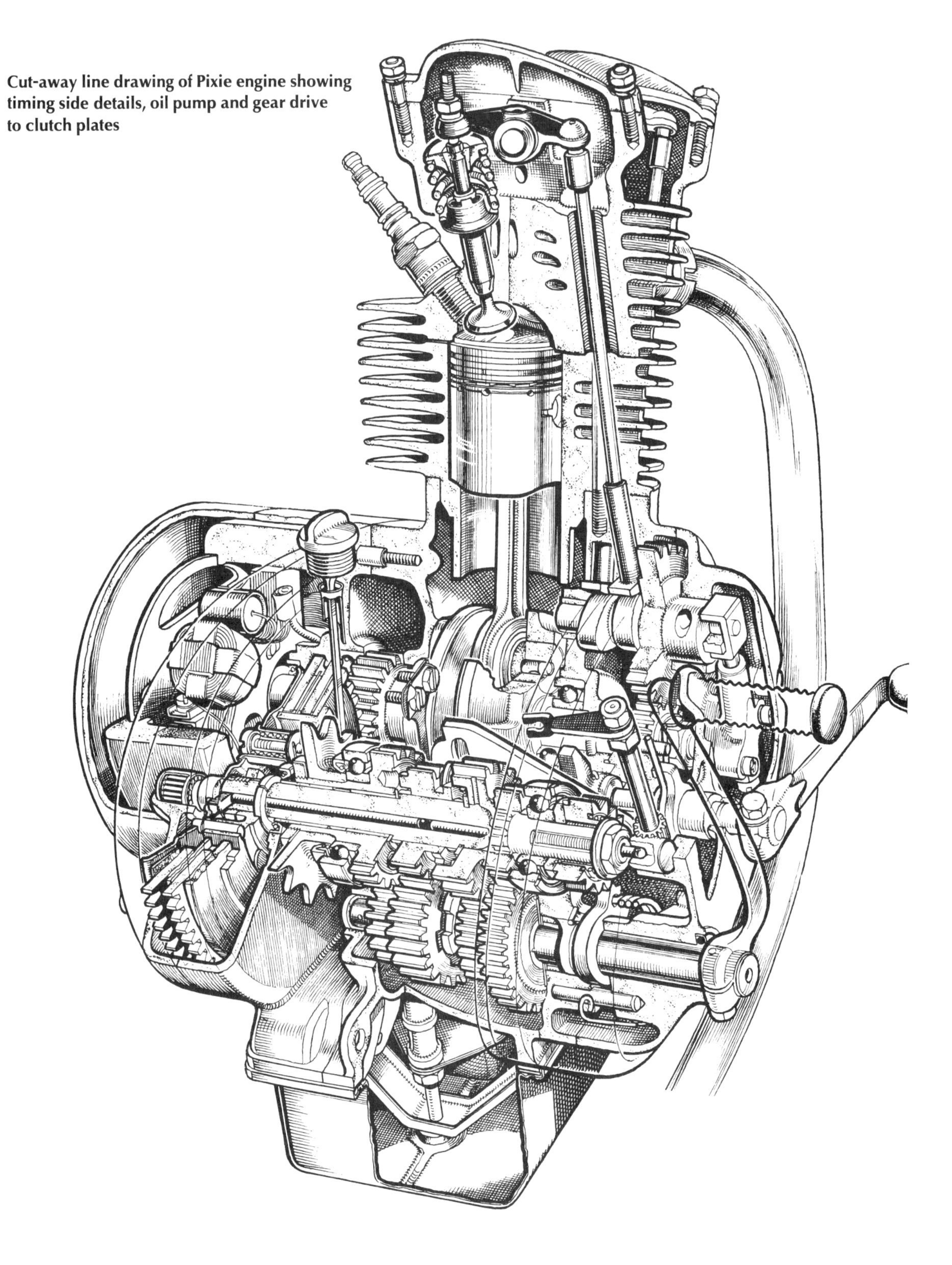

Cut-away line drawing of Pixie engine showing timing side details, oil pump and gear drive to clutch plates easily detached to allow the rear wheel to come out more readily.

In the spring of 1955 *Motor Cycling* road tested the Colt and in the main approved of the lightest Ariel mount. Maximum speed came out at 63 mph and on most journeys the model was cruised at 45 mph when it returned some 90 miles per gallon of fuel. The machine had good brakes and the front suspension worked well, but the movement at the rear was limited and thus a saddle might have been an improvement on the standard dualseat.

The engine was an easy starter using either the normal or the emergency circuits and the electrics provided an adequate headlight beam and good stop and tail rear light. The riding position was good but would have been improved if the bar ends had come back a little further, while the gearchange pedal was too far forward and perhaps also too high. These were, however, fairly minor criticisms and in general the report concluded that the Colt was well made, well finished and well suited to its tasks.

For 1956 there were two changes, neither of which looked sensible. The first was to two separate switches for the electrics, one for ignition and one for the lights and this made the wiring much simpler so was an improvement, although it seemed to be a complication. The second change was to the inlet tract and ran completely against the theories of gas flow for the tract was given a right-angle bend so the carburettor faced the right. It retained the air filter which faced the offside and looked most odd, but the firm claimed good results.

About this time a Colt was modified a little for trials use and gained good publicity for the Ariel name as it was ridden by Geoff Duke, and not without success.

1957 brought detail changes only with an ammeter appearing in the headlamp shell between the two switches and a new rear lamp being fitted. A new petrol tank of revised construction replaced the older style so the flutes went and a central band appeared. The battery strap was chrome plated and the finish changed to two-tone with the frame and forks in the original Brunswick green and the petrol and oil tanks, mudguards and toolbox in a light green. In addition the timing case, cylinder head fin edges and the rocker box cover were polished and an optional finish in deep claret was offered.

A further *Motor Cycling* road test confirmed the earlier findings and in this form the model ran on for a further two years until late in 1959 when it was dropped, along with the rest of the four stroke range.

At that stage it seemed that Ariel were firmly committed to their new two stroke models with a common engine. They were also becoming more subject to the dictates of the main group, and late in 1962 it was announced that the Selly Oak factory was to close and the machine production transferred to the BSA works at Small Heath. Thus more separate identity was lost.

Signs of the restraints that the group applied had been seen back in 1959 when a couple of Ariel models designed by Val Page and under development, were brought to a halt. One was an in-line four described in the next chapter, but the other was an interesting lightweight of 50 cc. As conceived by Page it had an overhead camshaft engine with both camshaft and primary drive by toothed belts so showed yet again his advanced thinking.

At the same time BSA were working on a small four stroke to replace the 125 cc Bantam and once the Ariel project became known it was ordered from high level that the Ariel should use a smaller version of the BSA engine which was designed by Edward Turner.

Thus were born the BSA Beagle and Ariel Pixie and although Page was forced to use the Beagle engine design, the Pixie chassis was totally Ariel. The two engines shared a common stroke of 42 mm and the Pixie had a bore of 38·9 mm to give its capacity 50 cc, while the Beagle was bored to 47·6 mm and 75 cc.

The single cylinder was inclined well forward and the engine and gearbox were built into one unit with wet sump lubrication. The crankcase was split vertically on the centre line of the cylinder but the whole of the gearbox was contained in the right half. The box end cover was carried forward on the right side of the case to form the timing cover.

The cylinder was iron and spigoted into the crankcase, while the head was die-cast in aluminium complete with rocker boxes. The rockers lay across the head with adjustors at the valve end and the timing side was a simple gear pair, a camshaft, tappets and solid alloy push rods.

In the bottom half the crankshaft was built up with a plain big end and flywheels pressed up

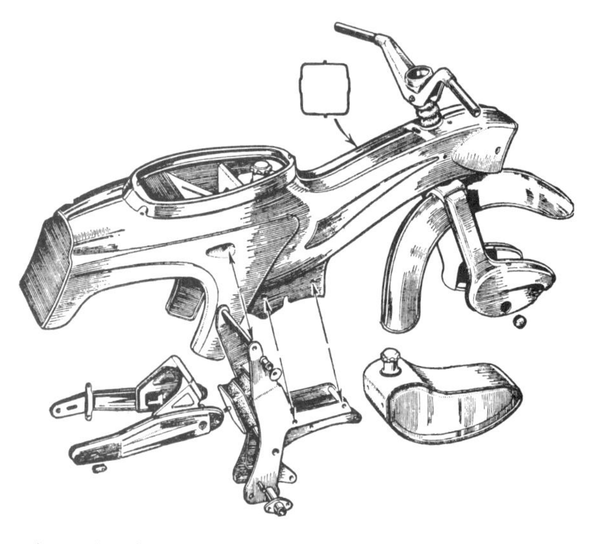

Above **Pixie frame construction with hidden fuel tank, subframe and rubber rear suspension**

Below **Pixie on show late in 1962, in this case fitted out with screen, basket, panniers and rear rack**

with the crankpin. Ball races on each side supported the assembly with a third race outboard of the gear primary drive, but with the flywheel magneto outside this on the left. The sump bolted to the base of the crankcase and a single plunger oil pump was driven by the crankshaft and fed the major bearings, rocker gear and primary drive.

The clutch and gearbox were modelled on others used by larger machines in the group and the transmission provided four speeds in the traditional manner with the output sprocket on the left. Kickstart and gear pedal went on the right and the clutch was lifted by a rack and pinion mechanism and a push rod running through the mainshaft centre. The primary drive was unusual in that the clutch friction plates had the gear teeth cut on them so no clutch drum was needed.

This engine unit went into a frame built up from steel pressings welded together and with a style similar to that of the two stroke range. The main shell comprised two main pressings and stretched from the headlight at the front to the rear numbler plate mounting. It thus formed the main beam of the spine above the engine, accommodated the petrol tank, supported the seat and gave a measure of enclosure to the rear wheel.

The engine itself was bolted to a sub-frame which also carried the rear fork pivot, supported the rear suspension unit, and carried the footrests, centre stand and brake pedal. This subframe was bolted to the main frame at three well spaced points so that the two could be easily parted for maintenance.

The rear fork was built up from pressings and a cross member which acted against the suspension unit. This was a block of rubber which worked in both directions and was secured to the sub-frame. At the front more pressings formed the front forks with short trailing link suspension arms. These moved within enclosures formed at the fork leg ends and were bellcranks pulling on rods that ran through the circular rubber suspension blocks. As the wheel rose the action was for the pair of blocks on each side to be compressed.

All the bearings in the suspension worked on nylon bushes so that maintenance was cut to a minimum. The head bearings were set in the main frame pressings and a single steering column rose from the lower crown with the handlebars attached bicycle fashion so their height could be varied. The bars themselves were made from a central pressing, which had provision in its centre for an optional speedometer, and tube grips. A substantial front mudguard was bolted to the underside of the fork crown with provision for the front number plate on the sides of its deep valances.

The hubs contained 4 in. brakes front and rear and the tyre size was 2·50 × 15 in., so the wheels were quite small. Knock-out spindles were used for both, and a full rear chaincase was specified. The front brake torque arm was slotted so it could rise with the wheel to maintain brake geometry, and again a nylon bearing was used.

The headlight unit was fitted into the front end of the main frame and the petrol tank was rubber mounted in the middle. The seat hinged up and beneath it were the filler cap, battery for parking lights, tyre pump and tool tray. The exhaust pipe and silencer went on the right side, low down.

A range of accessories were shown with the Pixie when it was first announced and comprised legshields, screen, mirrors, panniers and luggage carriers for front and rear of the machine.

Unfortunately this was rather premature for tooling was still being made at that point late in 1962 and it was a year later before the production models began to leave the line. They ran on through 1964 and into 1965 without change, but in the middle of that year their production was stopped.

This was part of a larger picture and the Ariel company was subject to the whims of the overall group board. They had been forced out of their traditional home and to drop their traditional line-up of models. Their fresh ideas for the future were either blocked or distorted and in the end the Ariel company was just put down with a humane killer. To many observers the horse was nobbled, kept on short rations until ill, and then given the coup de grace.

Some years later the respected Ariel name was linked to an abortive attempt by the BSA group to produce a special form of moped. This occurred in the middle of 1970 and was the result of a massive market research exercise carried out for the group which was then in serious difficulties on all fronts. Group finances had taken a downhill trend, management teams had grown out of all proportion to the size of the business, and the opinions of those who knew the motorcycle and its market were ignored.

This Pixie has a different badge by the headlamp, folding kickstart lever and revised carburettor and air filter

Out of this came the Ariel 3 and the best advertising slogan that it could generate was 'Here it is. Whatever it is.' which just about summed up the project. The idea was to offer the convenience of the moped with the stability of three wheels to promote safety, easy parking and economy.

The layout of the machine exploited a clause in the English regulations that allowed a pair of wheels to be counted as one if set close enough. Thus by restricting the rear track of the Ariel it

Right **All Italian Ariel built around 1968 with 160 cc Minarelli engine. A possible Bantam replacement, only this prototype ran before the project was abandoned**

Below **Infamous Ariel 3 that cost BSA so dear, demonstrates its split personality**

Here it is. Whatever it is.

It's not a bike. It's not a car. But it's fun. Ariel 3. Three wheels and a motor. Everyone's thought of the idea, no one's been able to make it work.

Until now.

The secret is the suspension. Tri-Torque suspension. A unique twin torsion-bar pivot system that lets you lean around corners, yet keeps the back wheels glued to the ground. Whatever you do.

Try it for yourself. There's a tough 50cc engine to give you push. And 4" diameter internally expanding drum brakes to stop you again. Then there's an automatic centrifugal clutch, and no tricky gears. So driving is easy. And a lot of fun.

If you want to know more, read on. Engine : single cylinder 2-stroke, 1.7 bhp, with 8mm reed induction carburettor, flywheel magneto, toothed belt primary drive, chain secondary drive, 12.55 overall reduction. About 125 mpg.

Suspension : trailing link front with micro-cellular polyurethane blocks for shock and rebound load damping. Tri-Torque twin torsion bar rear for banking control. Self righting.

That's it. Ariel 3. The handiest thing on three wheels. Takes one rider and 50 lb. of luggage. And puts a lot of fun back into your life.

Just you try it and see.

It's fun

Ariel 3, Armoury Road, Birmingham 11.

The best the ad-men could do as exemplified by this *Motor Cycle* **advert of July 1970**

could be classed as a moped, as then defined, which basically called for 50 cc maximum engine capacity and pedalling gear.

The trick of the 'trike' was that the front half could be banked over to negotiate a corner while the rear part stayed upright. To this end the front wheel, forks, pedals, front frame and saddle were treated as one unit, and the two rear wheels, engine unit and transmission as a second. The two were joined by a pivot on the machine axis and twin torsion bars on the same axis lifted the front end up when the corner was passed and held the machine upright when parked. Less publicized was their effect when the inside wheel ran over a bump in the road or a kerb, for this wound up the spring which reacted against the front half and tried to pick it up.

The power unit was a Dutch built 50 cc Anker two stroke mounted above the rear axle. It drove via an automatic clutch and toothed belt to a countershaft which contained a dog clutch to allow the engine to be disengaged if the machine had to be pedalled home. On the end of the crankshaft outboard of the drive belt was a cooling fan and the drive pinion incorporated a sprag clutch to enable the pedals to turn the engine over to start it.

Two trikes that reached Bermuda for renting to visitors where their performance was adequate for the island's 20 mph speed limit

Only the left rear wheel was driven or braked, and a chain connected it to the countershaft. A second chain ran forward to the pedals with various guides and pulleys to tension it and prevent it coming off the sprockets when the front end was lent over. The right wheel was fixed to a dummy live axle and was without a brake but all three wheels were fixed to the hubs on three studs, car-style, and could be interchanged.

The mechanics at the rear were supported by a large alloy fork which pivoted on a cross rod carried in a trunnion and the torsion springs acted as the suspension medium as well as holding the front end upright. They could be adjusted with screws to suit the preload to the rider's weight.

The front frame was built up from pressings and carried a trailing link fork with rubber suspension. The front brake was the same size as the rear and the tyres were 2·00 × 12 in. Dunlops on the pressed steel wheels.

Legshields were built on to the front end and a windscreen offered, while at the rear the panelling could be hinged up to give access to the engine. When down, this hood also enclosed the petrol tank but the filler cap protruded through the top so was accessible on the forecourt. A

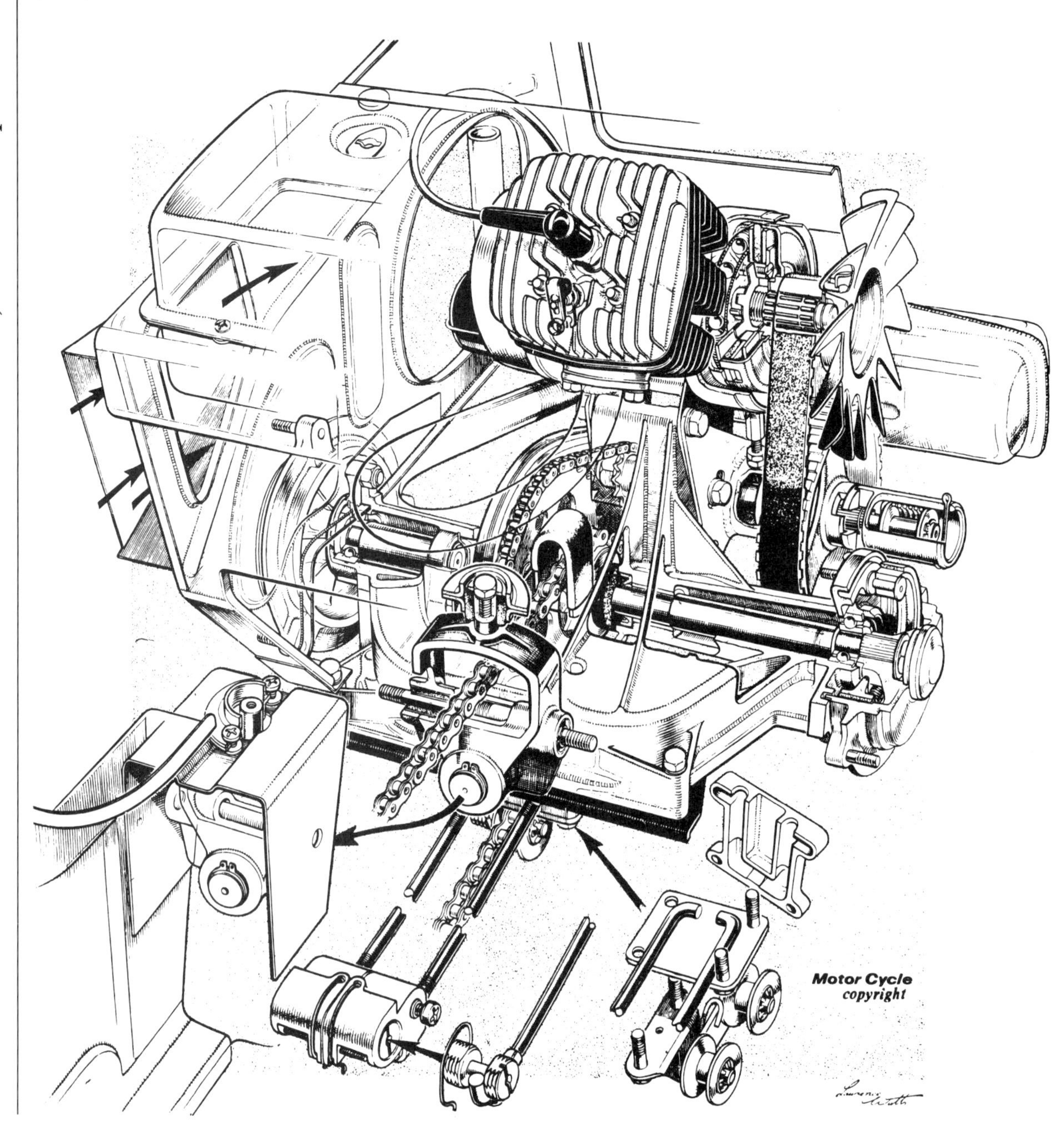

Line drawing of the trike's mechanics showing engine, transmission and cooling fan at the rear with the torsion bars, their adjustors and their location below the main pivot point

Side view of a financial disaster brought on by poor market research and unsound engineering

shopping basket with cover could be fitted on top of the hood but may have got rather warm from the engine.

It was an odd looking device but BSA had persuaded themselves that they could build and sell 2000 a week. Production was set up on this basis and the machine given a lavish and costly launch. Then the reports began to filter back of instability, poor engine reliability, bad starting, and many detail criticisms. Top speed was barely 30 mph and fuel consumption around 120 mpg, so poor by moped standards, and the ride was peculiar.

The '3' rapidly turned into a disaster and a flop. Only a few hundred were sold so all the expensive tooling was of no use, and as quickly as it had appeared it vanished. BSA were left with many, many thousands of engines which were sold off to the trade for very small sums and in all the exercise was said to have cost the group £2 million. It certainly was a real factor in the BSA collapse in 1972.

Years later, in 1982, the machine form (less the torsion bars) reappeared as the beautifully styled but very expensive Honda Stream.

At the time the use of the Ariel name for such a device was seen as an insult to all who had cherished the horse over the years, whether as users or makers.

6 Leader and Arrows

In the middle 1950s the Ariel range was very typical of the English industry and most models had a very long established pedigree. They lined up, model for model, with their opposition and only the Four lacked a counterpart among the BSA, Enfield, AMC and Triumph models in the showrooms side by side with the Ariels.

It was time to plan for the future. The problems of the immediate postwar period were well past and it would have been easy to settle into a steady canter as the years rolled along. This was not Ariel's way and at that time they were still able to operate much on their own with little interference from the main BSA group.

They also had a strong management team at Selly Oak headed by Ken Whistance, an ex-TT rider and production expert, who had the drive to fight off any group intrusion. Val Page had a lifetime of experience of motorcycle design and had showed many times his ability to ignore convention or use it to suit the needs of the job and his wide range of thought. To sell the resultant machines there was Tom Davis who had been with Ariel since the twenties and knew the problems of launching anything that smacked of the unconventional and non-conforming. To help him there was Bert Perrigo from BSA, although Bert soon returned to his spiritual home in Armoury Road. For all that his input must have been valuable.

The first problem was to decide what the machine of the future should be, thinking ahead some five years, for it would take that long to design, develop, test and put into production any machine that really was new. It was sensible to choose that long a timescale for it ensured that any thought of using existing parts for expediency could be safely pushed to one side. It also gave time to think about the design, time to test it properly and time to carry out the development before the tooling had to be committed. Only those who have been through the process fully appreciate the problems involved and the importance of holding back at times.

To answer the basic question, the firm tried some market research and the only common feature that came from that was for a 250 cc twin cylinder, two-stroke engine. Continental Shows were visited and trends studied and from this came the conviction that the only way to achieve a good price was to spend on tooling and use pressings, die-castings and plastics. Any process that gave finished or near-finished parts in one operation merited investigation and those that did not were to be used only in the last resort.

Early Leader days, a mock-up in the Ariel development department showing lines much as finally used

Two examples of their thinking concerned the petrol tank and the frame. The first was then expected to be a major styling feature and hold fuel despite vibration and the sheer weight of that liquid. A plain box was a tenth of the cost and an outer shell gave more freedom to the stylist. With the frame the process of forging lugs and then brazing cut lengths of tube into them sent shudders up a production man's back. Welded pressings were used for cars and mopeds, so why not for motorcycles?

The use of die-castings was easier to accept for the industry was turning to this process. It gave accuracy that could be repeated with the minimum of machining where this was essential. It was a far cry from the messy and laborious business of sand casting with its core boxes, pouring, fettling and heavy machining which produced mountains of swarf. Plastics were still new to many but again the one-shot thermoplastic materials were beginning to be better known and gave considerable advantages in price, consistency and finish.

So Val Page laid down the design of his new 250 assisted by Bernard Knight and Clive Bennett, who did the development testing. The result was the Leader and its existence was one of the best kept secrets of all time in the industry. There were odd leaks but nothing really serious. Some

April 1957 and Ken Whistance with pipe and Val Page smile with satisfaction. Machine name was then 'Glida', it changed later

tests were carried out in Wales using all black machines without any insignia, but when the testing was over the local postman congratulated the team on the new Ariel! Correspondence with the factory had been in the normal envelopes carrying the Ariel crest. On another occasion an Ariel tester stopped to help a rider stuck by the roadside. The man in trouble was an ex-road racer who worked for a company who made a two-stroke twin and learnt, under a pledge of secrecy, that his helper was indeed astride an Ariel. The secret was kept long after the Leader appeared.

The new machine was announced in the motorcycle press on 17th July 1958, and created an instant sensation. It offered a 250 cc twin engine, full enclosure, built-in legshields and screen, pressed steel beam frame and many unique features. A whole range of accessories were offered and a choice of two-tone finishes was listed. Even the nuts and bolts were brought up to date by the use of Unified threads on all the standard fixings, this being well before metrication was thought of.

Peter Howdle and Cyril Quantril, then *MCN* editor, with a Leader on a 24 hour test for the magazine

The basis of the machine was a large section, beam frame from which the engine and gearbox unit hung. The rear wheel fork pivoted from both the frame and the gearbox shell and the front suspension was by trailing links. The structure of the machine was then enclosed by panels with one a dummy fuel tank which was used for luggage stowage. A dualseat was fitted as standard and the wheels were smaller than usual.

The engine unit was a twin cylinder two-stroke with equal dimensions of 54 mm and a capacity of 247 cc. The two cylinders were parallel and inclined forward at 45 degrees with the firing interval at 180 degree. The engine porting was conventional for the period with inlet at the rear of the cylinder, exhaust at the front, transfers to each side of each bore and all timings piston controlled. Only one carburettor was fitted and the design was to preclude the easy fitting of dual units, although this was to be done in later days.

The engine and gearbox were both assembled into a single light alloy gravity die-casting which weighed 15 lb in its machined state. This one casting formed the two crankcases for the engine with a central dividing wall and both were open at their outer end. The front of the cases was well finned for cooling and the barrel mounting face a single machined surface into which eight studs, four per barrel, and the two barrel spigots went. Angled transfer cut-outs were cast into both of these spigot holes.

From behind the crankcase region rose a lug which was one of the mounting supports but it was given a second job to do as well. Its rear face was machined to take the carburettor and the lug was cored out to be hollow and form

Below **The trailing link forks used by both Leader and Arrow with nylon bushes and special Armstrong units**

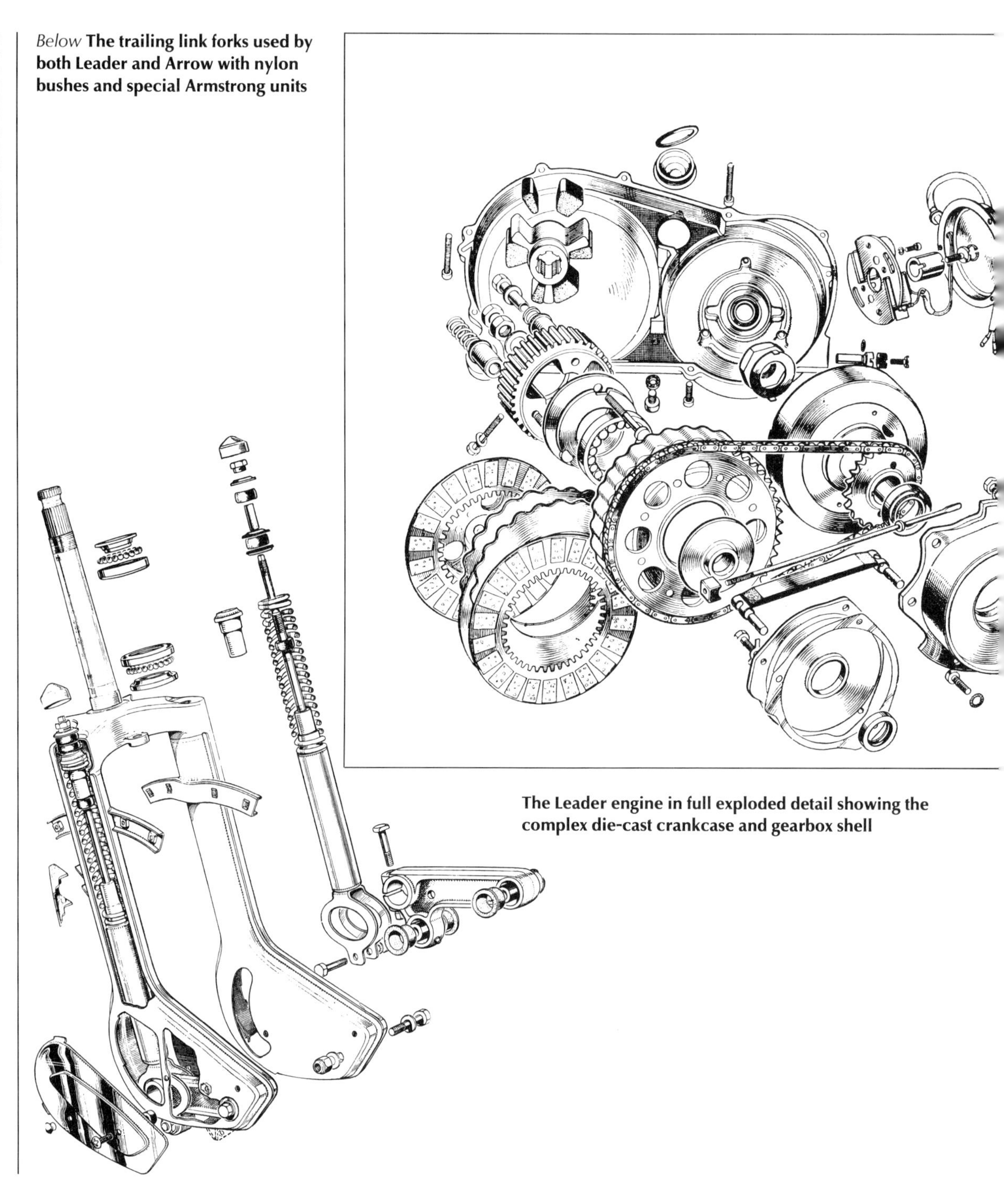

The Leader engine in full exploded detail showing the complex die-cast crankcase and gearbox shell

the inlet passage for the two cylinders. The tract split and ran to the rear of the barrel spigot holes where ports were formed. It was the presence of this lug and its supporting role that was to make the fitting of twin carburettors so difficult for private owners later on.

The crankcase was finned at the rear as well as the front for, although the gearbox shell was cast in one with it, there was an air gap between the two. On the left they were joined by a wall that formed the inner side of the primary chaincase and at the rear of this went extensions to enclose the rear sprocket and chain. The gearbox was open on the right in normal English fashion and that end was joined to the crankcase by a web. The line of this was run on behind the gearbox to form a pair of lugs with two large holes in them both of which carried bushes. On assembly to the frame the cross bolts were tightened and then the bushes locked with grub screws. The bolts themselves threaded into bosses cast into the final drive chain enclosure.

The great advantage of this complex casting was that it allowed the engine and gearbox to be dismantled without taking the unit out of the frame. In fact either cylinder could be stripped individually. The main snag was the need for the crankshaft to have a join in the centre and for the two crank chambers to be sealed from one another. This second aspect was dealt with by

The Leader in standard form as built from 1958–60 by which time its unusual style had become a common sight

mounting a single ballrace in the dividing wall and alongside this sat a pair of oil seals mounted back to back.

The split crankshaft need was dealt with in an ingenious fashion. The assembly for each cylinder was built up in conventional form by pressing the parts together. The flywheels were machined all over and balance obtained by drilling two holes in each web placed either side of the crankpin. As the engine was intended for touring these holes were not filled with light alloy although the machined flywheel running clearance was a mere 0·03 in. The mainshafts were formed in one with the wheels, while the crankpin was just pressed into place. The pin had a stepped diameter for the big end which comprised two rows of uncaged rollers running directly on the pin and in the big end eye of the connecting rod. A thrust ring went between the two rows and triangular thrust washers on either side.

The join between the two cranks was done

Left **Launch photo of Leader with accessories showing the false tank lid with its poor lock**

Above **Control layout of the standard Leader, headlamp lever in centre**

Above right **Layout when fitted with clock, mirrors, screen extension, turn indicators, neutral light and parking light**

Above far right **Turn indicators at the rear, a fitting not at first available**

Right **Panniers, indicators, bumper bar with reflectors and rear carrier did not stop the tail hinging up after releasing silencers from stays**

Far right **Under the seat went tools, tank cap, battery, seat lock and retraction tube for lifting bar**

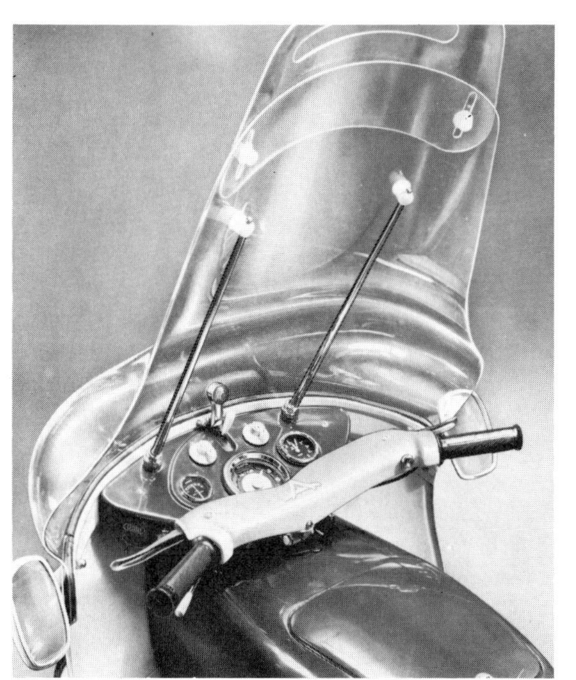

LUCAS

by mating tapers in the centre with a key to give the alignment. The tapers were held together by a substantial bolt with hexagon socket head and this was located in the hollow inner mainshaft of the right crankshaft. To enable it to be done up, the outer mainshaft was also hollow and allowed an Allen key to reach the bolt, and it was the need to clear this key with the connecting rod that determined the stroke of the engine.

The centre bolt pulled the two crankshaft halves together but a further problem then arose on dismantling with the need to force the tapers apart. This was overcome by fitting a circlip just outside the bolt head which first served to retain it and second gave the head something to push on as it undid. This was enough to push the two halves apart.

The crankshaft was supported at its outer ends by a ballrace which fitted, together with an oil seal, into a door. Each door was a tight fit into the side of the crankcase and sealed to it. A row of screws held the doors in place and tapped holes provided a pair of jacking points for their removal, further evidence of the thought that had gone into the design. The doors had fairly long spigots into the crankcase, which in part accounted for their tight fit, and were formed at the top to provide the lower end of the transfer passage. Holes from these points conducted oil mist to the main bearings and the centre race was looked after in the same way by a drain hole in the main casting. Lubrication of the engine was by petroil using a ratio of 25 : 1.

The connecting rods were ribbed round the big end eye and slotted for lubrication. They were of an I section and the small end was bushed to carry the hollow gudgeon pin retained by circlips.

Each piston had a slightly domed crown and gave a geometric compression ratio of 8·25 : 1. It carried two narrow rings and the gudgeon pin hole was offset by 0·062 in. to the rear to minimize piston slap. The piston had a transfer port cut on each side of the skirt beneath the pin hole.

Separate cast iron barrels were used, each deeply spigoted into the crankcase. Due to the depth of this the inlet port, which was bridged, was set in the spigot and thus connected with the passage cast into the crankcase. Transfer slots were cast into each side of the lower end of the spigot and the aim seems to have been to avoid loose edges of metal that could vibrate and create noise, even if this goal reduced the power a little.

Due to the depth of spigot the actual barrel length was very short and the wide spaced cooling fins were cast at an angle to it so as to be nearly parallel to the ground. The exhaust port was rather long to give an easy change from the rectangular port to the round pipe and to assist the pipe bend and fixing. Due to the heat feed back from this length, the original plan to have the fins at right angles to the bore had to be altered to the 10 degree inclination used.

The barrels were topped by separate cylinder heads die cast in aluminium alloy. Head gaskets were used and each head was held down by four sleeve nuts which screwed to short studs in the crankcase. The nuts had cap heads with a hexagon socket so the holes in the cylinder head were larger than the base studs to accommodate this, and the nuts served to align both head and barrel to the crankcase.

The combustion chamber was cast part spherical and had the plug positioned on the centre line with a 25 degree forward inclination. This gave good access for changing and suited the gas flow. At that stage no squish band was used. The head fins at first ran fore and aft, but after tests this layout was changed so that ahead of the plug they were angled to one side. This encouraged the air to flow in and over the combustion chamber and gave the castings a distinctive air.

In the lower half of the engine the hollow

Half a real Leader was fixed to the front of this works van and it made a fine advert for the model

NEW 250
ALL THAT THE NAME IMPLIES
ROOTES DIESEL
ALWAYS AHEAD
WOM 999

mainshaft on the right carried a Lucas alternator whose fixing bolt also sealed off the shaft. A pressed steel cover enclosed the stator. At the other end of the crankshaft went the primary drive sprocket and onto its boss was pressed and keyed a large external flywheel made in a close grained cast iron with most of the weight near the rim. This more than augmented the inertia of the internal wheels for its presence nearly doubled the figure for a relatively small weight increase.

Outboard of the flywheel went the outer half of the primary chaincase and this carried a further oil seal to protect the contact breaker points mounted on a plate on the outside. The points cam went right on the end of the crankshaft and the timing was fixed. To avoid the effects of shaft deflection due to chain pull the points cam followers were positioned above and below the cam so that any fore and aft movement would not affect the gap. A small outer cover kept the weather off them.

The ignition system was battery and twin coils with an emergency circuit to pass all the generator output to the right side only. The only items

The Arrow derived from the Leader by removing the panelling and providing a new seat and false tank. Very popular

that were to give owners' problems were the fixed points which prevented individual timing of the cylinders and the wiring colour code. The first could be overcome by juggling the points gap, or even splitting the points plate if you were really fussy. The second was more an irritation as the wires were black with white or yellow tracer, and in time these became hard to distinguish.

The primary drive was by a single strand endless chain to a wet clutch. The chain was adjusted by a steel blade faced with synthetic rubber which was pulled into an arc below the bottom run by a long rod screwed into a nylon block. The rod was accessible from the front of the chaincase.

The clutch was conventional in many ways with the sprocket and drum running on uncaged rollers, a shock absorber in the clutch centre, two plain plates and two with inserts bonded to them. The pressure plate also had inserts and was clamped in place by three springs. The unusual feature of the clutch was the drum. Instead of the normal slots it was formed into a corrugated shape with the plain plates to suit and thus had 24 driving faces and no problems with distortion. The clutch centre was made with gear teeth to transmit the drive rather than splines and thus more surfaces shared the load. The clutch was lifted by a simple lever with adjuster and locknut positioned on the right of the gearbox, which moved a push rod working through the gearbox mainshaft.

The gearbox was made by Burman and typically English in its layout. The mainshaft sat above the layshaft and ran in ball races with the sleeve gear concentric to it and carrying the final drive sprocket on the left. Access to this was gained by first removing the clutch and then a plate carrying an oil seal. The layshaft ran in bushes and one end drove the speedometer gear and its cable. Gear selection was done with flat plates attached to sliding rods and these had cross pins at their right end. The pins engaged

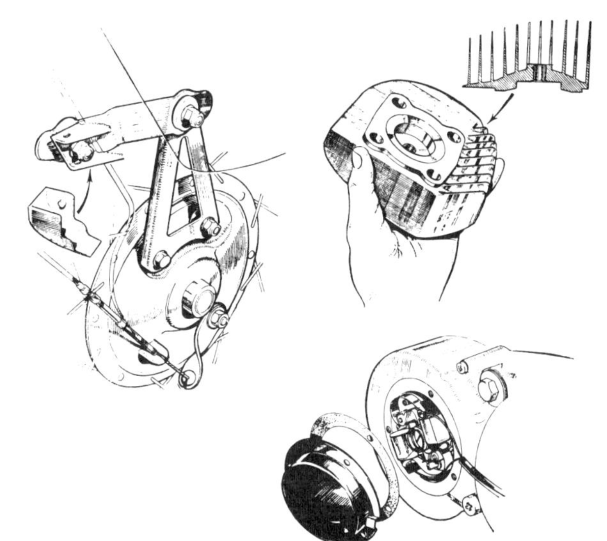

Changes for 1961 included a remote front brake anchorage, a new cylinder head with squish band and central plug, and a small points cover change

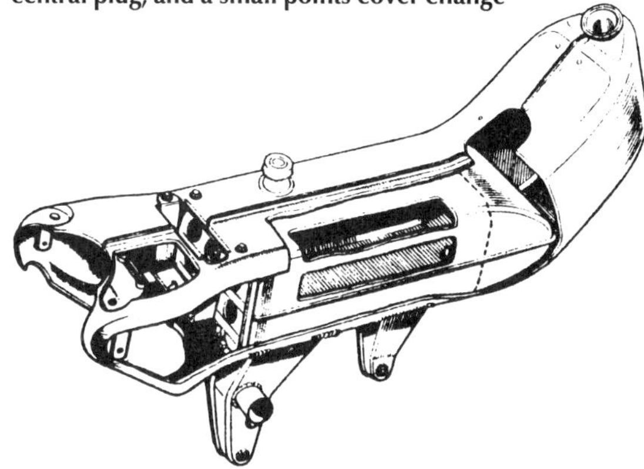

The common beam frame with the enlarged petrol tank, earlier ones stopped at the dotted line

with the cam track of the barrel drum and this was directly turned by the positive stop mechanism. Detents in its rear face held the gears in mesh and the drum had a dimple in its periphery to work an optional neutral light switch, if fitted. The kickstarter mechanism comprized a face ratchet on the end of the mainshaft which was turned by a quadrant on the pedal spindle.

The gears were contained in the main casting

with an inner end cover carrying the support bearings. This was closed off by an outer cover and in the resulting chamber went the change mechanism and kickstarter gears. Both covers were die-cast and the outer carried the clutch arm and a small cover giving access to its adjus-

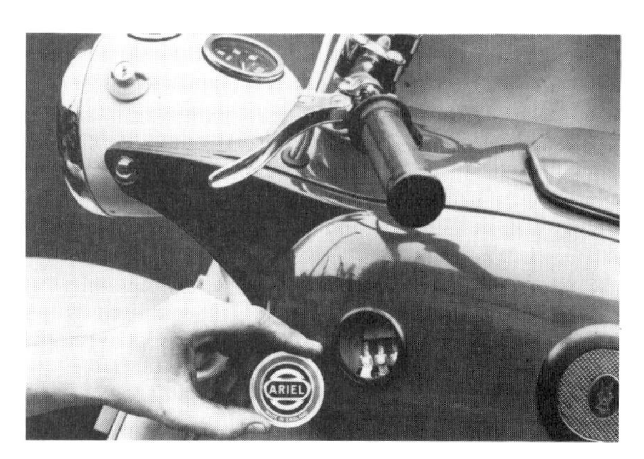

Right **Detachable badge on the Arrow gave access to the rectifier wiring**

Below **1960 Arrow fitted with legshields which was not too easy to arrange. Neat installation**

ter and a means of filling the gearbox with oil.

The whole engine and gearbox unit was hung from the main frame and this was built up from 20 swg pressings, welded together into a box form. This swept up and narrowed at the front to embrace the head bearings, while the tail flared out a little to support the rear suspension units. The tail was open ended to allow the fuel tank to be slid into the body of the frame. The tank was simply a box with internal baffles and was mounted on rubber. Its filler stuck up through a hole in the main frame and the cap was in plastic and also acted as an oil measure. It was sited beneath the seat which hinged up for access.

The tank was followed into the frame by a bracing plate behind it, and aft of that was a recess for the 6-volt battery to drop into. Right at the back went a heavier pressing bolted in to spread the loads from the rear units and the same bolts secured a tool tray on top of the frame.

Beneath the main box hung the engine mountings. The forward pair were roughly above the centre of gravity of the unit so it could hang from them, while the single rear mount was deeper. It contained two welded-in cross tubes to support the engine unit and the lower fixing bolt also acted as the rear fork pivot. The two bolts simply screwed into the engine casting but the pivot was locked by one of the primary chaincase screws which ran into it for added security. The support member also acted as the intake air silencer so had a stub welded into the right side to carry the drum-type air filter. A hole in the front was connected with a rubber hose to the carburettor, which was a conventional Amal Monobloc fitted with a butterfly choke with remote operation.

The rear fork was built from pieces of D-section tubing welded together and pivoted on bonded rubber bushes. One would have expected pressings as on the larger machines, but no doubt the limited tooling purse was unable to run to that. The pillion footrest lugs were welded to the fork arms so the passenger's feet rose and fell a little over the bumps, but this was an effective way to avoid a further subframe for this job.

The squish cylinder head adopted in 1961, note the large fixing holes for the sleeve nuts

Armstrong units controlled the rear fork and, while the lower ends had the usual eye end, at the top was a single central stud in line with the unit. This assembled to the frame with an assortment of steel and rubber washers and so followed car practice.

The rear fork also carried the two halves of the pressed steel full chaincase. This was not a sealed unit but did overlap at the join so kept virtually all the dirt at bay. Lubrication of the rear chain was from the primary chaincase and done with a wick feed. This was supplied from a small well filled by splash and allowed the oil to pass slowly through a nipple onto the chain.

At the front went a trailing link suspension system hidden inside pressings which formed the main fork legs. No top crown was used and the headstem was brazed into a massive malleable casting to which was also brazed the fork legs built up from 16 swg pressings. At the lower end these pressings extended forward to support the fork links.

1961 Leader with accessories, very little changed from its 1958 debut

The links were die-cast in a heat treated aluminium alloy and pivoted on nylon bushes. The wheel spindle went at the aft end and the links were extended below spindle level to form a further eye. This connected to the bottom of the Armstrong units which controlled the wheel movement and which were concealed within the fork leg pressings. The units anchored into the top crown in the same manner as the rear legs using washers and nuts.

This design gave the machine a nearly constant wheel base and also minimal angular movement for the suspension units. To allow the units to clear the wheel spindle they had special fork ends welded to them with oval holes to give the room needed. The fork end pressings also had holes in them for access and these were covered with styled panels. To ensure that the wheel spindle aligned with its access hole the pressings and the links were provided with holes and the toolkit contained two rods to hold the parts where needed.

Both wheels had knock-out spindles and light alloy, full width hubs with 6 in. brakes. These used the normal fulcrum adjusters common to the range and the rear hub was attached to its sprocket by three studs. Access to these was by removing a rubber plug from the chaincase and wheel removal also meant detaching the rear

He's out of luck for his Player's as the shop is closed but the Arrow is smoking enough for two anyway

brake rod and the torque stay. The brake rod was on the right and the pedal on the left so a cross shaft was needed, and this ran in a tube pressed into two lugs cast into the underside of the gearbox shell. As well as supporting the shaft, this tube acted as the bearing for the centre stand. The underside of the engine carried the separate footrests, each held on three studs, and one of these studs also held an exhaust pipe on each side.

At the front, the brake backplate was anchored by a floating link with near parallelogram layout. The link used part-spherical nylon bushes at each end to accommodate both fork movement and any misalignment of the parts.

Both wheels were of 16 in. diameter with 3·25 in. section tyres. The front was of the ribbed pattern and both had white walls. Both wheels were protected with mudguards but of very different types. The front guard was deeply valanced so carried the front number plate on its side and was made in two sections to fit front and rear of the fork legs on welded-on stays. At the rear the guard was short and plain and barely ran back past the top of the tyre.

This then was the basic structure of the Leader and onto it went the outer clothing which gave the machine its style and special form. This took the form of eight main pressings all in 20 swg

steel which together gave it a body, enclosure, legshields and screen base.

The main outer shell went around and above the frame and comprised a dummy tank running back to the dualseat base. The tank was used for carrying luggage so had a lockable lid in its top surface. Inside it and bolted to the frame was a simple steering lock with a steel pin working in a nylon moulding and this was not one of the machine's successes as the moulding would fracture easily.

The shell carried kneegrips and the seat hinged on the right. Beneath it went tools and the fuel cap and the opening in the body was braced with a cross tube containing a pull-out machine lifting handle.

The tail section was hinged to the main shell by a pivot bolt on each side. It extended out over the rear number plate surface formed in it and was reinforced internally. It gave a measure of enclosure to the rear wheel and hinged up to allow that item to roll out when needed. To allow it to do this its support to the tail ends of the silencers was made to be easily detached.

On each side of the machine went enclosure panels each held by five captive screws and the panels were slotted for the pillion footrests. Access holes allowed the choke lever and petrol tap to emerge but the gear pedal and kickstart lever had to come off before the right panel could be removed.

At the front of the side panels went the legshields and these bolted to the main frame at the top and a cross bracket at the bottom. The same bracket also took one of the side panel screws and was itself bolted to the crankcase.

A front cowl joined the tops of the legshields and ran up the front of the main shell. It carried an instrument panel and also acted as the support for a moulded perspex screen formed to provide hand clearance on full lock. The panel carried the speedometer in the centre with an ammeter on the left and an Ariel badge on the right. This could be replaced by an optional eight-day clock. Ahead of the instruments went the ignition and lighting switches, warning lights for neutral and indicators if fitted, and in the middle a small lever which raised or lowered the headlamp shell to alter the beam direction.

The headlight itself was mounted in a front cowl with spring washers to allow the shell to pivot. Behind it went the horn. The screen was supported by a pair of rods held by self aligning socket mountings in the instrument panel and nylon mouldings at the top. The handlebars were clamped to the top of the steeing column with serrations for alignment and were tubular with a pressing to cover the cables and just leave the grips exposed.

Under the cover went the wiring and on the right a stop light switch worked by the front brake lever to supplement the rear brake one, then a very rare feature. The bars were designed to take the turn indicator switch on the left so that this extra could easily be added.

Beneath both the shell and the engine went the exhaust pipes which were chrome plated but not polished, and twin silencers ran back to the rear of the machine. These were polished as they were on view and incorporated one of the fixings for the side panels. The silencer ends were cast alloy and finished off with plated dome nuts.

Power output was 16 bhp at 6400 rpm and tests showed the removal of screen and legshields reduced the maximum speed, when normally seated, by 4 mph. It went on sale in its own country at £209 11*s*. 7*d*. and was listed in a choice of two-tone finishes in red or blue with light grey.

A long line of optional extras was also offered. In addition to the indicators, neutral lamp and clock already mentioned, there was a parking

Left above **The Super Sports Arrow with special finish, dropped bars and flyscreen, better known as the Golden Arrow**

Left **Topping up the chaincase on a Super Sports**

lamp, inspection lamp, rear carrier, prop stand, front stand, pannier cases, pannier bags, trip speedometer and a waterproof cover for the dualseat.

It was an exceptionally enterprising design and, while it may have unsettled the more traditional Ariel enthusiasts, it was a very real pointer ahead. Ariel gave it a good launch and up to that moment kept it very firmly under wraps. Thus, although the trade and press knew the machine existed, no-one had an exclusive and the firm benefited by having the maximum impact from the launch.

Test rides soon followed and the machine was highly praised for its conception and execution. It was comfortable, went well, handled nicely and braked smoothly. Gear pedal movement was rather lengthy and as the operation was very light a much shorter travel would have been preferred. Top speed in one test came out at 69 mph and fuel consumption varied in proportion to the throttle opening with 73 mpg at a steady 50 mph.

Criticisms concerned the side panels which were not too easy to remove quickly, and the locking arrangements. Like the steering lock, the seat catch was mounted in the dummy tank and thus both depended on the security of the tank lid lock which failed to withstand any small penknife. From a quarter of a century on, the lack of any provision for electric starting, use of petroil lubrication and four speeds seems antiquated but were normal practice for the period.

Within the tight financial restraints the team had to work in, it was a great achievement.

There were no changes for 1959 to machine or finish, and in the middle of the year the extras list was augmented by a pair of mirrors. Around the same time it was revealed that in a back room at Selly Oak was a Leader engine fitted with two calibrated carburettors each served by its own fuel tank. The engine was in fact a test rig and used for comparative tests which could be run literally side-by-side.

Late in 1959 the traditional range of Ariel four-strokes had come to a stop leaving just the

Below **Arrow, Sports Arrow and Leader all turn together**

Right **Leaders on police duty escorting German Panzers in South Wales**

POLICE
POLICE

LUCAS

Left **The Leader in the form it was built from 1961 on to its end in 1965**

Far left **Police Leader with panniers and extra tank top equipment**

Left below **Shropshire Police Arrow with short seat, massive radio-telephone and extra large battery needed in those days**

Leader in the range. At the end of the year the range was doubled with the announcement of the Arrow, a more conventional version of the Leader stripped of its enclosure.

The basics remained the same with the engine and gearbox unaltered, the main frame beam supporting it and front suspension by trailing links. Different were the false tank top, the handlebars and the rear end treatment.

The engine unit was that of the Leader without change. A pressed steel panel was added to shroud the gearbox end cover and the alternator, and the air filter housing finish was altered to match that of the panel. The horn was moved to a point just ahead of the filter.

The main frame beam and the whole of the suspension system, the forks and the rear chaincase were straight from the Leader. At the rear of the main beam went a rear mudguard pressing which carried the rear number plate and a pair of supports for the silencers. While these items remained essentially the same as for the Leader, the exhaust pipes were bent differently and also polished before being chrome plated in the normal manner. Lifting handles were provided on each side at the rear of the main frame.

The seat went on top of the main beam and was again hinged. It sat down on rubber buffers and was held by a pair of clips to conceal the battery top and the filler cap. This last item was also new to the Leader and contained a ball valve to act as a vent while preventing fuel from spraying out. The tank itself remained unaltered although a larger optional one was mentioned as a possibility for both models.

Ahead of the seat went a dummy tank which was extended ahead of the steering column to support the headlight which carried speedometer, ammeter and both switches. The tank again was meant to carry luggage and in the access hole was dropped the tool tray. This was located by a cross bar which turned into slots to hold the tray, and a lid fitted over the top and was held by a single screw into the bar. The dummy tank carried kneegrips and round plastic badges and the left one detached to give access to the rectifier connections as this unit was positioned on the beam to be in a draft. The ignition coils remained where they were inside the beam with access via a hole with a pull-out cover.

The handlebars and controls were all conventional and held by a central clamp. The lower part of this was splined to the steering column in the same way as the bars on the Leader.

The Arrow hubs were the same size as the Leader but cast in iron as there had been one or two problems with the alloy ones cracking. The rear brake retained the fulcrum adjuster but at the front the lack of access to the brake forced a change to convention and a cable adjuster. The wheels and tyre sizes remained unchanged but the whitewall tyres were not fitted as standard, although offered as an extra.

The finish for the common parts remained in the light grey but the dummy tank, gearbox cover, silencer ends, air filter housing and fork spats were in dark seal grey. The price was £167 13*s* 5*d*.

One was quickly out on test and the lower weight of the Arrow enabled it to step off the mark a little more briskly than the Leader, and the indications were that it would be a little quicker. It cruised at 60 mph and returned around the same number of miles to the gallon of petroil if large throttle openings were maintained.

The handling and braking were also praised but in fact both were not really as good as they should have been. Up to 60 mph the machine sat well enough on the road but above that speed it began to pitch and weave. Fast, bumpy corners had to be treated with a degree of respect and shutting off in the bend aggravated the problem. Under power the tendency was held in check.

The brakes only ever felt to be just about adequate when riding solo. They never actually faded but there was the ever present feeling that they were on the point of doing so and heavy pressure on the controls was needed to stop from 70 mph. The addition of a passenger was definitely too much for them and braking for roundabouts had to start early. In all it indicated a need for a 7 in. drum to cope with the weight and speed.

Early in 1960 one Arrow was aimed at the summit of Ben Nevis. It was prepared and ridden by Sammy Miller and with him went Jeff Smith riding a trials C15 BSA. The Arrow had the gearing lowered, a 20 in. front wheel and 18 in. rear with 3·50 in. trials tyre. The footrests were moved back and the exhausts siamezed and connected to an upswept silencer.

Miller and Smith were both trials experts of the highest class and spent most of the January day struggling up the mountain. They did not quite manage the summit but came closer than most others could have reached. On two wheels it was quite an achievement.

Ariel policy was to modify only if necessary and to do it as they went along so several changes occurred during 1960. These were all confirmed for 1961 along with some more but most were really details.

In the engine, development and some involvement in racing had led to a change of head and rod. The cylinder head was new with a compression ratio of 10:1, squish band and central plug.

1962 outside the Ariel works with a line of screen-less Leaders fitted with indicators, panniers and parking lights

Due to the plug move the fins were altered a trifle and thanks to the changes the power was raised a little. The connecting rod section was changed to an oval to promote gas flow.

Other details concerned the clutch pressure which was reduced by fitting washers under the spring screws, a reduction in main jet size, and a groove in the points cover so it was no longer threaded on the two wires in their sheath. The silencer internals had been modified for the Arrow to make them easier to clean and maintain and this change went on to the Leader as well. It gave the exhaust gases a spiral motion and from then on both models became noted for leaving twin curls of smoke behind them, especially under acceleration.

The major change was to the front brake. The cable adjuster had become the norm and was backed by a double nipple at the cable end. This was a distance piece threaded on to the inner of a length so that when the brake was partly worn it could be moved from one side of the cam lever to the other so as to take up the wear. The brake anchorage was also changed to move the torque arm out to work at a larger radius and so reduce the load on it. To do this a bracket was fixed to the backplate and extended above the hub, while an anchor point was welded to

The Leader for 1963 with no changes from the year before and few in its five year life

the back of the fork leg. A small plastic cap was clipped on after assembly to conceal the fixing.

The hubs were also changed with both machines using a common pair cast in iron as on the Arrow but with three shallow external ribs to improve rigidity. Also common was a three gallon fuel tank without baffles and the extra capacity came by extending the forward end of the tank which meant moving the ignition coils. This tank had been an option for some months for either model.

On the Leader a trip speedometer became a standard fitment and the inspection lamp holder material was changed from brass to plastic. The turn indicators became available with revised mountings so they could be fitted to any Leader and not just one with panniers as before.

For the Arrow the colour options were extended to match the Leader but for ease of production this only affected the false tank, the other items remaining in seal grey.

The Arrow was joined by a brother very early in 1961 so that Ariel then had a stable of three two-stroke twins. The new model was officially called the Super Sports but, due to its finish, was immediately christened 'The Golden Arrow' by trade, press and public.

It was not just a new grooming, as the power was raised by the fitting of a larger bore carburettor. This increased the cross section area by some 47 per cent and pushed the power up to 20 bhp at 6600 rpm. The handlebars were changed for a dropped pattern and fitted with red pvc grips and ball-ended control levers. Surmounting the bars was a small plastic flyscreen and equipment fitted as standard included a folding kickstart lever, two-level petrol tap, propstand and whitewall tyres.

The finish really made the machine stand out as the dummy tank and rear number plate mounting were painted in polychromatic gold. The primary chaincase, kneegrip trim plates and silencer ends were polished and chrome plating applied to the gearbox cover, points cover, fork spats, toolbox lid, lifting handles and air filter body.

On test the added power pushed the top speed up to 75 mph and the overall consump-

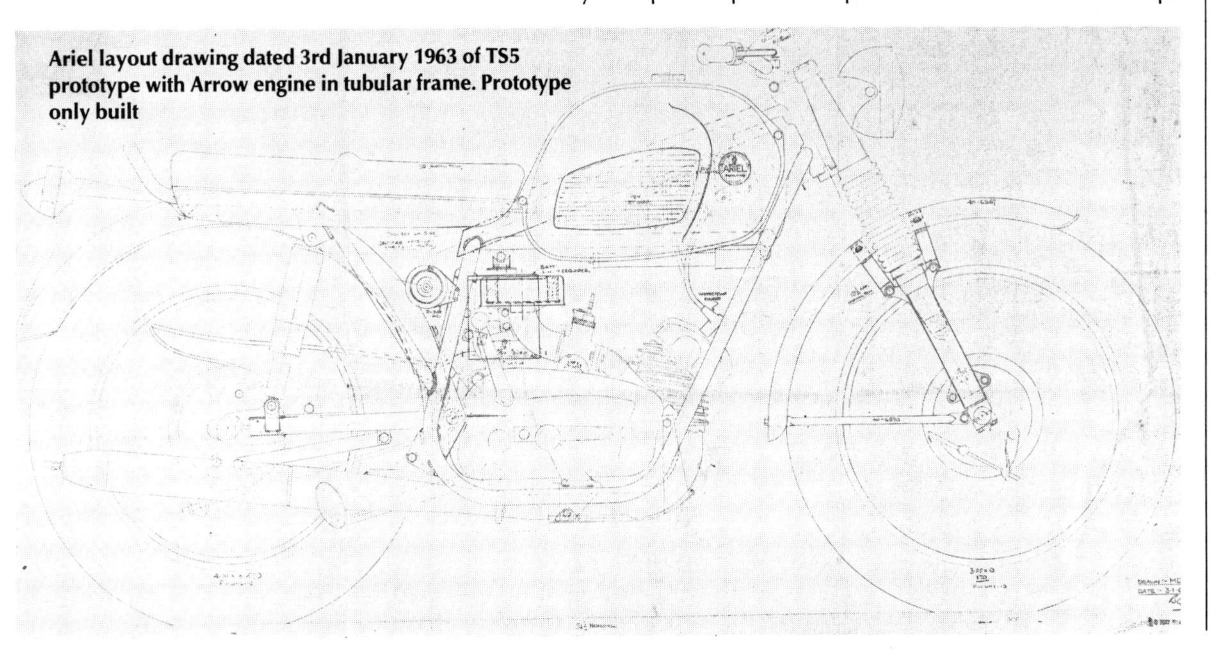

Ariel layout drawing dated 3rd January 1963 of TS5 prototype with Arrow engine in tubular frame. Prototype only built

The Arrow assembly at Small Heath after the transfer from Selly Oak

tion during a 500 mile test was 68 mpg. Acceleration was very brisk up to 60 mph when top gear had to be engaged but then faded rather, indicating the need for another ratio between the two upper gears. The front brake was thought to be marginal and the braking figures confirmed this. The gear lever travel was still rather excessive and the dropped bars compromised the riding position a little as their use really called for the footrests to be moved to the rear slightly.

The new version was as popular as the others for the Super Sport won the prestigious *Motor Cycle News* 'Machine of the Year' competition in 1961, as had the Arrow in 1960 and the Leader in 1959, the first year it was held. To hold the trophy with the same basic design for three years was a fine indication of the foresight of the Ariel company.

For 1962 there were colour changes and a new alternator type. This gave a few more watts at the top end but boosted the low speed output so making the life of the battery much easier in town. At the same time plug and socket connections were adopted between the harness and the two switches, while the ignition one became key operated.

The brake backplates gained a water-exclud-

Right **1963 Ariel advert for the Leader listing both the standard and optional equipment on offer**

18 APRIL 1963 MOTOR CYCLE 1

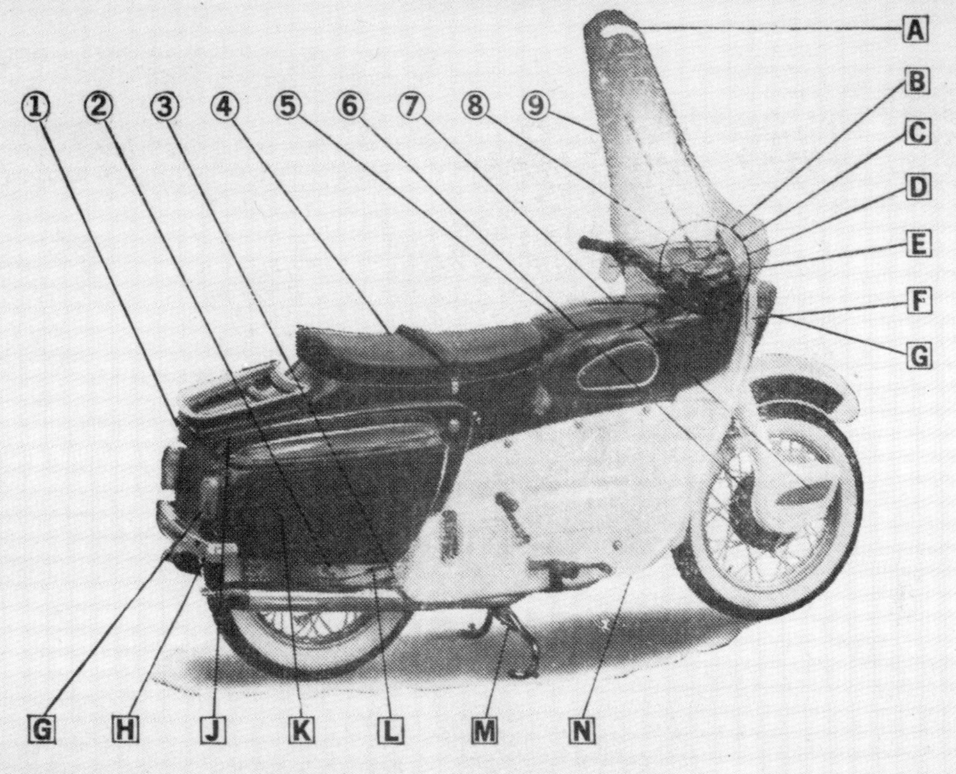

Only the LEADER has so much... offers so much

The most important thing about any motorcycle is the basic design. Ariel design is far ahead. Based on the rigid steel "chassis" that gives such a superb standard of road-holding and steering, it makes Ariel the *finest possible two-wheeled vehicle.*

But your pleasure and comfort in riding are enhanced by many thoughtful details. See what the luxurious Leader gives you as standard equipment. See the neatly designed features you can easily add, choosing just what you want. Isn't this the logical way to arrive at the perfect motorcycle for *you?*

LEADER £219.12.0 ARROW £192.0.0 ARROW SUPER SPORTS £206.8.0

Prices include purchase tax

TOMORROW'S DESIGN—TODAY!

Standard on the LEADER

1. Stoplight worked by either brake.
2. Quick-detachable wheels (complete tail unit hinges upward).
3. Totally enclosed rear chain.
4. Pull-out lifting handle.
5. Locking tank-top parcel compartment (steering and dualseat also lock).
6. Full-width hubs.
7. Nylon bushes on front and rear suspension pivots, no greasing needed.
8. Instrument panel with ammeter and trip speedometer.
9. Windscreen.

And other features that are often extras on other makes.

B Neutral gear indicator light.

C Parking lamp (low consumption).

D Plug-in inspection lamp.

E 8-day clock.

F Rear-view mirrors (pair).

G Flashing trafficators.

H Chrome rear fender with reflectors.

J Carrier.

K Locking pannier cases (also lift-out zip bags to fit).

L Supplementary heavyweight rear springs.

M Prop stand.

N Detachable front stand.

Designed accessories you can fit

A Slotted windscreen extension.

A wide choice of useful items! All of them fit right and look right because they're Ariel designed.

YOU SAVE ON INSURANCE!

ARIEL MOTORS LTD., BIRMINGHAM 11

Please send me your latest catalogue, and details of special money-saving "Clearway" Insurance rates available to Ariel owners.

NAME .... *Tick if under 16* ☐

(BLOCK LETTERS, PLEASE)

ADDRESS ....

.... L-MC-55

Refuelling the Sports Arrow when petrol was 5 'bob' a gallon. Wonder if he insisted on Castrol in his petroil

ing flange developed by Sammy Miller for the Leader hubs used in his trials machine and fitted to the front brakes for much of 1961. It went on to the rear also and both backplates were stiffened with internal ribs. While this improved that area it gave rise to brake squeal so springs to prevent this were added to all brake shoes. A louder horn was fitted to the Arrow.

The colour changes were from light grey to ivory for the bulk of the painted items on all models with the second colour for the standard Arrow black with no options. Fewer details had this finish, both the chaincase and fork spats

Sectioned Sports Arrow on show in 1963 with all the details exposed

Publicity photo of 1962 Arrow receiving a polish up

being in the ivory. The Golden Arrow retained its gold and chrome while the Leader had the black colour added to its list of options in red, blue or seal grey to go with the ivory.

Early in 1962 Leader reliability was demonstrated by a rider who took one along the 2325 miles of the Monte Carlo rally route from Paris to Monaco. Over the whole distance his riding average was around 35 mph which was good for French roads in January. The machine was fitted with many of the optional accessories plus a good sized spot lamp.

Another road test, this time by *The Motor Cycle*, saw a maximum of 81 mph for the Golden Arrow and repeated the comments on the riding position. Overall it received a good report with just one or two minor blemishes for rather silly faults such as a weak stand spring that allowed that item to clatter, and the fiddle of removing a lid, a crossbar and a box in order to get at the luggage.

In the middle of the year came news of an Arrow scrambler but this was a strictly private venture of Mick Burton from Malvern. He started with the normal engine which was mildly tuned with expansion boxes and fitted this to his own frame fabricated from 16 swg sheet steel. The beam was retained but in a different way and the petrol tank was made as part of the frame.

An Ariel rear fork and C15 telescopics carried the wheels which had Ariel hubs and a one-piece dummy tank, seat pan and rear mudguard moulded in fibreglass went over the frame.

There were no machine changes for 1963 but for the firm there were many, with the transfer of production to the BSA works at Small Heath. 1964 again left the three models alone mechanically but the standard Arrow gained a colour option in red and ivory.

The lack of change was in part brought on by the decline in motorcycle sales in general. The figure for 1963 was half the 1959 peak and after a small rise in 1964 was to run down until a revival in the early 1970s. The Mini was well established and offered an undreamed of level of sporting performance for the price, while the appearance of motorways brought a need for faster cruising speeds.

Furthermore, while the Leader and Arrow models had many very good points going for them there were also irritants that never seemed to be bothered with. The seat base rotted, the steering lock snapped off if the rider forgot he had engaged it and straightened the bars, the screen was an expensive replacement and very easy to break, the points had to be set just right too often, and cold starting was poor as the butterfly choke could not induce enough mixture into the engine.

On the credit side were many rider's features but the odd appearance and the details evened

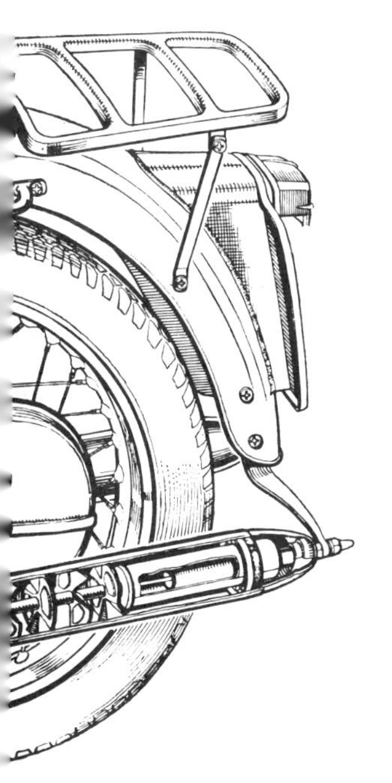

Above **The smaller capacity Arrow 200 built in 1964–65, little different from the 250**

Left **Line drawing of the Arrow in its first form with small tank and inclined spark plugs**

the scales too much. Thus not enough riders bought Ariel to enable the firm to push ahead with improvements and the effects of the move from the traditional Selly Oak stable must have been adverse.

In the middle of 1964 Ariel came up with a new version of the twin called the Arrow 200. This was a smaller capacity model aimed to fit into a lower cost insurance class and thus give riders an incentive to buy. The reduction was gained by cutting the bore size to 48·5 mm which gave a capacity of 199 cc. With this went a smaller Monobloc and two more teeth on the rear wheel sprocket to lower the gearing.

Otherwise it was standard Arrow but finished in British racing green or aircraft blue for the dummy tank and rear chaincase. The other painted parts were in their usual ivory and the tank carried special badges with 'Ariel 200 Arrow' on them.

On test it proved to have a performance not much slower than an Arrow at 71 mph and only really lost out a little on acceleration and hill climbing. Otherwise it was pure Arrow with all its good points and bad.

Engine unit of the prototype in-line four built into Leader cycle parts. Air cooled and single carburettor

Sadly its days were numbered along with the other models for in the middle of 1965 came the BSA decision to cease Ariel production. It was a time of great change in the British motorcycle industry and of many wrong decisions. It was the start of the great decline and Ariel were too small and without their traditional home so were unable to withstand the forces upon them.

The standard Arrow had been the first to go late in 1964 but the others soon followed. One of the official reasons given out was that Burman would no longer manufacture the gearbox, but in view of the gear shop at BSA this looked more like an excuse than a reason. In all some 36,000 twins were believed to have been made, split roughly between the Leader and the various Arrows.

The tragedy was that the formula was so right and could so easily have been developed on for the 1970s. More power, twin carburettors, six speeds, an oil pump and electric starting would have been easy enough for the factory to design in. Allied to a steady programme to rid the machine of the main complaints of poor gear-change and brakes this could have pushed the model along for many years.

Instead it went and with it died the house of

the horse, and into the same grave went several projects which indicated the versatile lines the company could think along if left alone.

The first of these was built as a replacement for the Square Four with the aim being to create a luxury tourer that was fast enough, use an under-stressed engine that was easy to maintain, and give the rider protection from the weather. To look after this last aspect the machine was based on the Leader chassis as this gave the desired result with a proven package.

Val Page laid out the design and decided that he needed 700 cc which, with a mild state of tune, would give an easy 90 mph and that four cylinders were required to give the smooth running looked for. As the chassis and side panels precluded a transverse engine he opted to run the crankshaft along the frame and to get it under the frame beam he laid it on its side. This place the cylinder head on the left and moved

Above **The in-line four with its twin headlights was well finished for a prototype**

Below **Shaft drive for the four with axle housing just clamped to fork leg and exposed joint and shaft**

the crankshaft enough to the right for a straight shaft drive to the rear wheel.

The engine was a perfectly conventional in-line four with overhead valves and single carburettor. It was all-aluminium to keep the weight to an acceptable level and was air cooled with a fan to help move the air along. Compression ratio and valve timing were mild so a broad spread of power could have been expected so that four speeds would have been enough. A car-type clutch drove the gearbox and a universal coupling connected it to the rear hub and its crown wheel and pinion.

A single exhaust system ran along on the left, while lubrication was wet sump and pressure fed to the three plain bearing mains and the big ends. Electrics comprised an alternator on the nose of the crankshaft, coil ignition and an electric starter.

The chassis was Leader modified to suit the engine unit and stiffened in places to take the extra power and weight. The front forks were the usual trailing link and at the rear the fork was altered to carry the bevel housing. The hubs remained standard but the wheels altered to 3·25 × 17 in. at the front and 4.00 × 16 in. rear. The bodywork required little change to suit, with just extra holes for the footrests and pedals. The most noticeable change was at the front where twin headlights were fitted side-by-side in a special housing that carried turn indicators on its sides and a single central parking light.

The new engine was not an instant success and suffered material problems with a porous head casting and design ones with oil drainage into the rocker box via the push rod holes which were set too low. However, these and other snags could have been developed out to give the aimed for smooth fast travel. As on the Leader, maintenance of the engine was easy for most of it could be dismantled from the side, in the frame. It was not a heavy machine either and compared well with contemporary big twins.

Only the one prototype was built but at least that progressed further than other design projects for a 250 cc four, a 350 cc triple two-stroke and a 350 cc parallel twin with belt driven camshaft all of which remained paper exercises only.

One machine that did reach the metal was a 350 cc parallel twin with overhead valves that slotted into an Arrow frame. The aim was to have a four-stroke to run alongside the two-stroke engine and to do this costs had to be kept down. The result was a well inclined engine laid forward

Above **Engine unit of 4 stroke Arrow prototype, 350 cc, twin cylinder and overhead valves**

Left **4 stroke Arrow used normal gearbox and fitted the format well but only one was built**

Home built Ariel Arrow triple, a very professional job to match the Japanese 3s. Badge from 'Ariel 3' came in useful

to fit under the frame beam with dimensions of 63 × 56 mm and a capacity of 349 cc. The camshaft ran across the engine behind the cylinders with the points set inside the timing cover. Wet sump lubrication was used with the sump extending forward between the two exhaust pipes and a single carburettor was fitted. Plain bearings were used.

The engine was mated to an Arrow gearbox and the chassis was pure Arrow down to the silencer brackets. The performance was typical of the type with vibration at the top end but a good spread of power at touring speeds. The design speed was 75 mph and the machine was built around 1960.

In later years the engine was tried in a tubular frame, as had an Arrow unit, but neither of these experiments came to anything and most finished up buried in the 'big hole in the floor' at BSA. Fortunately the 350 twin unit was rescued from going for scrap and was eventually rebuilt into an Arrow chassis.

The prototype Leader 4 also still exists along with the MkIV Square Four with its swinging arm frame. All the evidence suggests that the marque could have had a real chance of surviving if it had been allowed to stay in its original stable, unfettered by Small Heath, and if a replacement for Val Page, with his breadth of experience and forward vision, could have been found.

7 Competition

Ariel never won a TT or a classic road race but their machines, especially the Red Hunters, were part of the backbone of sporting motorcycling throughout the thirties, forties and into the fifties. When all their competition activity should have stopped they came back with a model which found itself in club races and more, while their obsolete single dominated the trials world for years.

The Hunter engine was tough, simple and easy to work on so a natural for those days when one machine was expected to compete with some degree of success in several branches of the sport and take its owner to work during the week. Even the side valve units of those days could and were pressed into action if nothing else was to hand.

As the Ariel single remained little changed in its essentials for so many years it was popular with clubmen as most parts were common, and it was easy to update an early machine. Furthermore, the design gave a good power output so the model was competitive.

Thus in the 1930s Red Hunters were to be seen in trials, scrambles, hill climbs, sprints and at Brooklands. Some of the most successful at the speed events were the machines tuned by Laurence Hartley and ridden by Jock West in prewar days, and Peter Ferbrache postwar, plus many others. The Hartley Ariels ran normally on alcohol fuel so the iron engine was no handicap, and in addition to the overhead valve models he also

Charles Howkins on the Square Four he rode in the 1948 Clubman's TT which retired on the first lap; he was 4th the next year

Peter Ferbrache on the Hartley Ariel at Brands Hatch in 1951 when one rode up Paddock Hill

prepared a side valve engined machine of 600 cc which ran at well over 90 mph on a methanol based fuel.

Less successful were various endeavours to wean more power from the Square 4. Early in this field were the Bickell brothers, Ben and Joe, who acquired a 600 in 1933 and reduced it to 500 cc with the 51 mm bore block. Their aim was to be the first all British team of man and machine to crack the 100 miles in the hour using a multi. To boost the power they fitted a blower and in time the machine lapped Brooklands at over 111 mph in a three lap race. Unfortunately the four resolutely refused to run for much longer without blowing the head gasket and all attempts to overcome this inherent weakness were to come to nought.

After the war a Square Four ran in the Clubmans TT for a couple of years ridden by Charles Howkins and, although he retired in 1948, the following year saw him fourth in the 1000 cc class. Of more news impact was the appearance of a much modified machine built for short circuit racing. What had begun life as a 1936 rigid 600 became a short stroke, water-cooled, supercharged 500 in the hands of Dick Foster-Pegg.

Most of the bottom half of this engine remained standard, but the crankshafts were remade to reduce the stroke and all the connecting rods made as stout as the best in the stock unit. The top half was all made from scratch with separate head and block, both encased in water-cooling jackets. The heads were all joined together and each went on to three studs in the block.

Twin superchargers, actually aircraft vacuum pumps, were mounted in front of the engine and driven by bevel gears from a cross-shaft. This was connected by chain to the front crankshaft which also chain drove a water pump. Two Amals were fitted, one for each blower, and the latter were lubricated by the original Ariel pump. A second pump driven from the far end of the cross-shaft looked after the engine.

The complete engine was fitted into what looked like a normal Ariel frame with telescopics and link suspension rear. In practice the frame also acted as the radiator with small bore pipes to bridge the lugs. Later on a header tank was added and the system pressurized, but it seemed to work quite well. It was not an immediate success but with good acceleration and a 100 mph top speed capability proved that its owner's ideas did work. Unfortunately in 1951 both he and it went to Canada.

Later users of the Square Four went for sprinting where the doubtful head gasket was less of a liability and just having 1000 cc in a lightened machine gave a good time for the period. Later came blowers once more, slick tyres and low minimal frames.

In the immediate postwar period 350 cc ex-WD Ariels were used for all manner of events. They were plentiful and could readily be tuned for any event using prewar aids as needed. The extra ground clearance of the model was a bonus for competition work and their tough breeding allowed them to be run for week after week with few problems.

Left **Square Four prepared for sprinting with four carburettors and mounted in Featherbed frame**

Below **The Healey sprint 4 with blower, stub exhausts and special low frame**

Frank Wilkins and Kay on their Ariel outfit in 1954, a very popular and successful combination

The make had little success in the late forties in the more important trials but at club level plenty of Ariels were in use, and in the ISDT Bob Ray upheld the firm's honour in the country's great years from 1948 to 1951, and in 1953. He rode in the Vase team the first and last years, and in the Trophy team for the others. In 1950 he and the other Ariel riders aiming for a makers' team award used 500 cc twins which were a little more special than they looked.

As always the machines abounded with features to speed up maintenance but in addition they were fitted with alloy tanks, despite the risk of a clutch lever puncturing them in those days before ball ends were usual. The gearboxes were modified and the front hubs in light alloy, but the most special feature was the incorporation of oil damping into the link rear suspension. This was fitted inside the main pillar on which the slider moved and, despite the small oil capacity, did allow the use of much softer springs which improved handling over the rough terrain. The riders carried small oil guns and topped the system up when needed and when they had time.

After the ISDT successes and some wins by Bob Ray in 1951, the works solos had several lean years but compensation came in the sidecar class. Soon after the war, in 1947, Frank Wilkins teamed up with Kay and they won their first event together, albeit on a Norton. In 1948 Frank returned to the Ariel marque he had ridden prewar and bought a machine rather typical of the era, a 1936 Red Hunter engine in an ex-WD chassis.

Army riders on Ariels prepared for the ISDT

The team of Frank, Kay and Ariel were immediately very successful in sidecar trials and by 1949 were receiving some assistance from the factory. They went on to win golds in the ISDT, the ACU Trials Star and the British Experts four times. And the publicity of an attractive lady passenger did not do Ariel any harm.

In 1956 Ron Langston joined the team to ride the new HT5 and at last some solo success came their way, and that year Sammy Miller had his first ride in the Scottish on the make. 1957 saw these two together with Gordon Blakeway to the fore of the solo results, while Wilkins and Peter Wraith took many sidecar honours.

From then on until the end of 1964 the solo trials world was completely dominated by Sammy Miller and his Ariel. On it he won the British Experts three times, the Scottish Six Days twice, and the Scott three times. The list of national events won was endless and several were taken for five, six or seven years in a row. It was an unmatched performance established in the face of factory disinterest after 1959 on a machine that became increasingly too large for the events it won. During this period Ron Lang-

Ron Langston, a great all-rounder on two wheels or three on his solo Ariel in the 1959 Scottish

19

ston turned from two wheels to three and was very successful, taking the British Experts in 1962.

When the Arrow was announced it was suggested that it would make a nice road racer, and it did not take long for this to happen. One of the first to prepare such a machine was Hermann Meier, a respected two stroke engineer, and the result was ridden by Michael O'Rourke under Harold Daniell's sponsorship.

The machine was given its first airing in April 1960 and set the pattern for many others that followed in club racing over the years. The heart of the work went into the engine and much of that was devoted to converting to twin Amal GP carburettors which fitted on to a plate bolted to the crankcase. To allow this to be done the original inlet port and mounting flange had to be cut away and filled in by welding. As this removed the engine support new cylinder heads were made incorporating lugs which bolted to a new bracket fixed to the frame beam.

For the rest it was an Arrow with the unwanted road gear removed, the wheels rebuilt into 18 in.

Above **Sammy Miller concentrating in the 1964 Manx Two Day trial**

Left **Peter Wraith in the 1962 Welsh**

Above **Peter Inchley on the George Salt Arrow he and Robin Good rode in the 1961 Thruxton 500**

Left **Racing Arrow with twin carbs and fitted into duplex tubular frame**

Right **Sammy Miller working on the Ariel Arrow he rode in the Welsh Two Day Trial; it lost some gears and he was forced to retire**

85 CESD
695 AOH
51

The Ariel 4 built up from two Arrow engines by Ernie Earles. Later outdone by the V-12 unit now in Donington Museum

rims, and expansion boxes fitted. It made a promising debut and in the TT came home a creditable 7th, the first private model, at 80·18 mph. Over the next few years the Meier Arrow was copied by others, although the problem of fixing the twin carburettors remained an awkward one for most people. Because of this a good few ran with a single unit and the standard inlet port, but this considerably restricted the power.

While the Meier Arrow was interesting, the sidecar outfit wheeled out by Ernie Earles for Bill Boddice late in 1960 was a sensation. It was a full 500 with two Arrow engines mounted side by side with a central coupling driving a Norton racing gearbox. Both engines were mildly tuned and fitted with twin GP carburettors and expansion boxes. Coil ignition was used with a battery in the sidecar nose and a distributor on the right end of the engine.

The initial tests showed the machine to be competitive and it was further modified for 1961. Larger Amals were fitted with the appropriate attention to the breathing of the internals and also an early form of electronic ignition developed by Lucas. The resulting extra power narrowed the rev-band so the engine ran best between 7000 and 8000 rpm and this emphasized the need for a five- or six-speed gearbox. Unfortunately minor problems prevented the machine from doing much and in practice for the 1962 TT, where it was driven by Ron Langston, it broke a rod.

A little earlier another Arrow made its mark in the sprinting world. It was ridden by George

Above **An Arrow converted to disc inlet valves for road racing**

Below **Antony Brown with the sprint Arrow minus any form of streamlining**

Brown, sometimes to relieve his tensions if Nero, his big Vincent, played up, and broke British records for both standing and flying start quarter miles. Flying it was good for over 130 mph and took the record as 126·64 mph.

It carried on something of a tradition of sprint success for a 250 cc Ariel, for in the middle to late 1950s John Terry was a frequent class winner with one such. His machine was a single and based on a 1939 trials model. The engine was warmed up although it kept to petrol, the weight cut down and AMC telescopics added.

It contained perhaps the essence of what was so good about the classic Ariel single for so many years. The ability to be competitive in so many fields with the same basic design aided by patient and careful work by the owner and tuner.

They sure did breed them tough in Selly Oak.

Appendix

Specifications

Model	4F	4F/600	4F/600
Year from	**1931**	**1932**	**1939**
Year to	**1932**	**1936**	**1939**
Bore (mm)	51	56	50·4
Stroke (mm)	61	61	75
Capacity (cc)	498	601	599
Compression ratio (to 1)	5·8	5·8	6·9
Valve position	ohc	ohc	ohv
inlet opens BTDC	10	10	25
inlet closes ABDC	50	50	55
exhaust opens BBDC	55	55	60
exhaust closes ATDC	15	15	20
Valve clear. (cold) in. (in.)	0·002	nil	0·006
Valve clear. (cold) ex. (in.)	0·004	nil	0·008
Ignition timing (in.)	0·312	0·312	0·187
Points gap (in.)	0·012	0·012	0·012
Front tyre (in.)	3·25 × 26	3·25 × 26	3·00 × 20
Rear tyre (in.)	3·25 × 26	3·25 × 26	3·25 × 19
Brake front dia. (in.)	7	7	7
Brake rear dia. (in.)	7	7	7
Front suspension	girder	girder	girder
Rear type	rigid	rigid	rigid
Petrol tank (Imp. gal)	2·5 **1**	3·12	3·25
Oil tank. (Imp. pint)	4 **2**	5	6
Ignition system	magneto	magneto	magneto
Generator type	dynamo	dynamo	dynamo
Battery (Volt)	6	6	6
Wheelbase (in.)	55	55	54·5
Ground clear. (in.)	4·5	4·5	4·75
Seat height (in.)	26·5	26·5	26·5
Width (bars) (in.)	30	30	30
Length (in.)	86	86	86
Power: bhp		24	23
@ rpm		6000	5600

1 1932—3·12. **2** 1932—5.

Model	4G	4G Mk 1	4G Mk 2
Year from	**1937**	**1949**	**1953**
Year to	**1948**	**1953**	**1959**
Bore (mm)	65	65	65
Stroke (mm)	75	75	75
Capacity (cc)	995	995	995
Compression ratio (to 1)	5·8	6·0	6·7 **1**
Valve position	ohv	ohv	ohv
inlet opens BTDC	25	25	25
inlet closes ABDC	55	55	55
exhaust opens BBDC	60	60	60
exhaust closes ATDC	20	20	20
Valve clear. (cold) in. (in.)	0·006	0·001	0·006
Valve clear. (cold) ex. (in.)	0·008	0·001	0·008
Ignition timing (in.)	0·312	tdc	tdc
Points gap (in.)	0·012	0·015	0·015
Front tyre (in.)	3·25 × 19	3·25 × 19	3·25 × 19
Rear tyre (in.)	4·00 × 18	4·00 × 18	4·00 × 18
Rim front	WM2	WM2	WM2
Rim rear	WM3	WM3	WM3
Brake front dia. (in.)	7	7	7
Brake front width (in.)	1·12	1·12	1·12 **2**
Brake rear dia. (in.)	7	7 **3**	8
Brake rear width (in.)	1·12	1·12 **3**	1·25
Front suspension	girder **4**	teles	teles
Rear type	rigid **5**	rigid **6**	rigid **7**
Petrol tank (Imp. gal)	3·9	3·5 **8**	5
Oil tank (Imp. pint)	6	6	6 **9**
Ignition system	magneto	coil	coil
Generator type	dynamo	dynamo	dynamo
Output (Watts)		70	70
Battery (Volt)	6	6	6
Wheelbase (in.)	54·5	56	56
Ground clear. (in.)	4·75 **10**	5	5·5
Seat height (in.)	26·5 **11**	28 **12**	30 **13**
Width (in.)	30	27	27
Length (in.)	86	86	86
Dry weight (lb)	420	412 **14**	425 **15**
Power: bhp	36	34·5	40 **16**
@ rpm	5800	5400	5600 **16**

1 7·2 option, standard from 1954. **2** 1956—1·5. **3** 1951—8 × 1·25.
4 1946—teles. **5** 1946—link option. **6** link option. **7** link option, standard from 1954.
8 1951—3·75, 1952—4·0. **9** 1956—8. **10** 1948—5. **11** 1948—28. **12** 1950—29.
13 1956—31. **14** 434 with suspension. **15** 1954—435. **16** 42/5800 with 7·2: 1 compression ratio.

Model	KG 500	KH 500	KHA	FH
Year from	**1948**	**1948**	**1952**	**1954**
Year to	**1951**	**1957**	**1953**	**1959**
Bore (mm)	63	63	63	70
Stroke (mm)	80	80	80	84
Capacity	499	499	499	647
Compression ratio (to 1)	6·8	6·8 **1**	6·8	6·5
Valve position	ohv	ohv	ohv	ohv
inlet opens BTDC	15	15	15	30
inlet closes ABDC	55	55	55	70
exhaust opens BBDC	46	46	46	65
exhaust closes ATDC	20	20	20	25
Valve clear. (cold) in. (in.)	0·002	0·002 **2**	0·005	0·010
Valve clear. (cold) ex. (in.)	0·002	0·002 **3**	0·008	0·010
Ignition timing degree	30	30	30	34
Points gap (in.)	0·012	0·012	0·012	0·012
Front tyre (in.)	3·25 × 19	3·00 × 20 **4**	3·00 × 20	3·00 × 20 **4**
Rear tyre (in.)	3·50 × 19	3·50 × 19	3·50 × 19	3·50 × 19
Rim front	WM2	WM2	WM1	WM1
Rim rear	WM2	WM2	WM2	WM2
Brake front dia. (in.)	7	7	7	7
Brake front width (in.)	1·12	1·12 **5**	1·12	1·12 **5**
Brake rear dia. (in.)	7	7	7	7
Brake rear width (in.)	1·12	1·12 **5**	1·12	1·12 **5**
Front suspension	teles	teles	teles	teles
Rear type	rigid **6**	rigid **7**	rigid **6**	s/a
Petrol tank (Imp. gal)	3·25 **8**	3·25 **8,9**	4	4 **9**
Oil tank (Imp. pint)	5	5 **10**	6	6
Ignition system	magneto	magneto	magneto	magneto
Generator type	dynamo	dynamo	dynamo	dynamo
Output (Watts)	36 **11**	36 **11**	56	56
Battery (Volt)	6	6	6	6
Wheelbase (in.)	56	56	56	56
Ground clear. (in.)	5	5 **12**	5·5	5·5
Seat height (in.)	28 **13**	28 **13,14**	30	31
Width (in.)	27	27	27	27
Length (in.)	86	86	86	86
Dry weight (lb)	375	378 **15**	370	410
Power: bhp	24	26 **16**	28	35
@ rpm	6000	6500 **16**	6200	5750

1 7·5 option, standard from 1954. **2** 1952—0·005. **3** 1952—0·008. **4** 1955—3·25 × 19.
5 1956—1·5. **6** link option. **7** link option, 1954—s/a. **8** 1950—3·75, 1951—4·0.
9 1957—4·5. **10** 1952–6. **11** 1949—56. **12** 1954—5·5. **13** 1950–29. **14** 1954–31.
15 1954—390. **16** 1954—28/6200.

Model	W/NG	NG	NH	VB
Year from	**1940**	**1945**	**1945**	**1945**
Year to	**1945**	**1950**	**1959**	**1958**
Bore (mm)	72	72	72	86·4
Stroke (mm)	85	85	85	102
Capacity (cc)	346	346	346	598
Compression ratio (to 1)	6·5	6·0 **1**	6·0 **1,2**	5·0 **3**
Valve position	ohv	ohv	ohv	sv
inlet opens BTDC	5 **4**	22	22 **5**	22
inlet closes ABDC	55	70	70	70
exhaust opens BBDC	60	70	70	70
exhaust closes ATDC	20	25	25	25
Valve clear. (cold) in. (in.)	nil	nil	nil **6**	0·003
Valve clear. (cold) ex. (in.)	0·002	0·002	0·002 **7**	0·006
Ignition timing (in.)	0·375	0·375	0·50	0·312 **8**
Points gap (in.)	0·012	0·012	0·012	0·012
Front tyre (in.)	3·25 × 19	3·25 × 19	3·00 × 20 **8**	3·25 × 19
Rear tyre (in.)	3·25 × 19	3·25 × 19	3·25 × 19	3·25 × 19
Rim front	WM2	WM2	WM1	WM2
Rim rear	WM2	WM2	WM2	WM2
Brake front dia. (in.)	7	7	7	7
Brake front width (in.)	1·12	1·12	1·12	1·12
Brake rear dia. (in.)	7	7	7	7
Brake rear width (in.)	1·12	1·12	1·12	1·12
Front suspension	girder	girder **10**	girder **11**	girder **10**
Rear type	rigid	rigid **12**	rigid **12,13**	rigid **12,14**
Petrol tank (Imp. gal)	2·62	2·5	2·5 **15**	3·25 **16**
Oil tank (Imp. pint)	4	4	4 **17**	6
Ignition system	magneto	magneto	magneto	magneto
Generator type	dynamo	dynamo	dynamo	dynamo
Output (Watts)		36 **18**	36 **18**	36 **18**
Battery (Volt)	6	6	6	6
Wheelbase (in.)		56	56	56
Ground clear. (in.)	6	6 **19**	5	5
Seat height (in.)		28 **20**	28 **21**	28 **20**
Dry weight (lb)	354	348	348	365
Power: bhp	17	13 **22**	17 **23**	15 **24**
@ rpm	5800	5000	5800 **23**	4400

1 1947—6·2. **2** 1956—7·5. **3** 1952—6·0. **4** 1940—3, 47, 52, 12 **5** 1951—26, 77, 70, 33. **6** 1952—0·006. **7** 1952—0·008. **8** 1949—0·25. **9** 1955—3·25 × 19. **10** 1947—teles. **11** 1946—teles. **12** 1947—link option. **13** 1954—s/a. **14** 1955—rigid or s/a, 1956—s/a. **15** 1951—2·75, 1954—4·0, 1957—4·5. **16** 1951—3·5, 1954—4·0, 1957—4·5. **17** 1953—6. **18** 1949—56. **19** 1950—5. **20** 1950—29. **21** 1950—29, 1954—31. **22** 1950—14·2. **23** 1950—19·4, 1956—18/5600. **24** 1950—15·5, 1952—17.

Model	VG	VH	VCH	VHA
Year from	**1945**	**1945**	**1949**	**1952**
Year to	**1950**	**1953**	**1953**	**1953**
Bore (mm)	81·8	81·8	81·8	81·8
Stroke (mm)	95	95	95	95
Capacity (cc)	499	499	499	499
Compression ratio (to 1)	6 **1**	6 **1**	6·8 or 7·5	6·8
Valve position	ohv	ohv	ohv	ohv
inlet opens BTDC	22	22 **2**		26
inlet closes ABDC	70	70		77
exhaust opens BBDC	70	70		70
exhaust closes ATDC	25	25		33
Valve clear. (cold) in. (in.)	nil	nil **3**	nil **3**	0·006
Valve clear. (cold) ex. (in.)	0·002	0·002 **4**	0·002 **4**	0·008
Ignition timing (in.)	0·375	0·50	0·50	0·50
Points gap (in.)	0·012	0·012	0·012	0·012
Front tyre (in.)	3·25 × 19	3·00 × 20	3·00 × 21	3·00 × 20
Rear tyre (in.)	3·25 × 19	3·25 × 19	4·00 × 19	3·25 × 19
Rim front	WM1	WM1	WM1	WM1
Rim rear	WM2	WM2	WM3	WM2
Brake front dia. (in.)	7	7	7	7
Brake front width (in.)	1·12	1·12		1·12
Brake rear dia. (in.)	7	7	7	7
Brake rear width (in.)	1·12	1·12		1·12
Front suspension	girder **5**	girder **6**	teles	teles
Rear type	rigid **7**	rigid **7**	rigid	rigid **8**
Petrol tank (Imp. gal)	3·25	3·25 **9**	2·5	3·5
Oil tank (Imp. pint)	6	6	4	6
Ignition system	magneto	magneto	magneto	magneto
Generator type	dynamo	dynamo		dynamo
Output (Watts)	36 **10**	36 **10**		45
Battery (Volt)	6	6		6
Wheelbase (in.)	56	56	54	56
Ground clear. (in.)	5	5	5·5 **11**	5·5
Seat height (in.)	28 **12**	28 **12**	30	30
Width (in.)	27	27	27	27
Length (in.)	86	86	84	86
Dry weight (lb)	375	375	300	364
Power: bhp	22	24·6	25	24·6
@ rpm	4600	6000	6000	6000

1 1947—6·8. **2** 1951—26, 77, 70, 33. **3** 1952—0·006. **4** 1952—0·008. **5** 1947—teles. **6** 1946—teles. **7** 1947 link option. **8** link option. **9** 1951—3·5. **10** 1949—45. **11** 1952—6·5. **12** 1950—29.

Model	VH	HS	HT 1	HT 3
Year from	**1954**	**1954**	**1954**	**1957**
Year to	**1959**	**1959**	**1959**	**1959**
Bore (mm)	81·8	81·8	81·8	72
Stroke (mm)	95	95	95	85

Model	VH	HS	HT 1	HT 3
Year from	**1954**	**1954**	**1954**	**1957**
Year to	**1959**	**1959**	**1959**	**1959**
Capacity (cc)	499	499	499	346
Compression ratio (to 1)	6·8	9·1	5·6	5·6
Valve position	ohv	ohv	ohv	ohv
inlet opens BTDC	26	50 **7**	26	26
inlet closes ABDC	77	70	77	77
exhaust opens BBDC	70	67	70	70
exhaust closes ATDC	33	47	33	33
Valve clear. (cold) in. (in.)	0·006	0·010	0·006	0·006
Valve clear. (cold) ex. (in.)	0·008	0·010	0·008	0·008
Ignition timing (in.)	0·50	0·50	0·50	0·50
Points gap (in.)	0·012	0·012	0·012	0·012
Front tyre (in.)	3·00 × 20 **2**	3·00 × 21	3·00 × 21 **3**	2·75 × 21
Rear tyre (in.)	3·25 × 19	4·00 × 19	4·00 × 19	4·00 × 19
Rim front			WM1	
Rim rear			WM3	
Brake front dia. (in.)	7	7	7	7
Brake front width (in.)	1·12			
Brake rear dia. (in.)	7	7	7	7
Brake rear width (in.)	1·12			
Front suspension	teles	teles	teles	teles
Rear type	s/a	s/a	rigid **4**	s/a
Petrol tank (Imp. gal)	4 **5**	2·5	2·5 **6**	2
Oil tank (Imp. pint)	6	4	4	4
Ignition system	magneto	magneto	magneto	magneto
Generator type	dynamo			
Output (Watts)	56			
Battery (Volt)	6			
Wheelbase (in.)	56	56	53	53
Ground clear. (in.)	5·5	6·25	7	7
Seat height (in.)	31	31	32	32
Width (bars) (in.)	27	27·5	27	27
Length (in.)	86	84	80	80
Dry weight (lb)	375	318	290	285
Power: bhp	26	34	24	
@ rpm	6000	6000	5800	

1 1957—HT 5. **2** 1955—3·25 × 19. **3** 1957—2·75 × 21. **4** 1956—s/a.
5 1957—4·5. **6** 1956—2·0. **7** Mk III—37, 70, 62, 45.

Model	LH	Pixie	Ariel 3
Year from	**1954**	**1963**	**1970**
Year to	**1959**	**1965**	
Bore (mm)	60	38·9	40
Stroke (mm)	70	42	38
Capacity (cc)	198	50	48
Compression ratio (to 1)	7·5	8·8	7·0

Model	LH	Pixie	Ariel 3
Year from	**1954**	**1963**	**1970**
Year to	**1959**	**1965**	
Valve position	ohv	ohv	2 stroke
inlet opens BTDC	34 **1**	35	
inlet closes ABDC	78	53	
exhaust opens BBDC	74	60	
exhaust closes ATDC	38	32	
Valve clear. (cold) in. (in.)	0·001 **2**	0·003	
Valve clear. (cold) ex. (in.)	0·002 **3**	0·003	
Ignition timing (in.)	0·06	0·135	
Points gap (in.)	0·015	0·012	
Front tyre (in.)	2·75 × 19 **4**	2·50 × 15	2·00 × 12
Rear tyre (in.)	2·75 × 19 **4**	2·50 × 15	2·00 × 12
Rim front	WM1 **5**		
Rim rear	WM1 **5**		
Brake front dia. (in.)	5·5	4	4
Brake front width (in.)	1		
Brake rear dia. (in.)	5	4	4
Brake rear width (in.)	0·62		
Front suspension	teles	trailing link	trailing link
Rear type	plunger	s/a	torsion bar
Petrol tank (Imp. gal)	2·5	1·12	0·75
Oil tank (Imp. pint)	4	1·5	
Box capacity (Imp. pint)	0·5	0·38	
Ignition system	coil	magneto	magneto
Generator type	alternator	alternator	alternator
Output (Watts)	48	21	
Battery (Volt)	6	6	
Wheelbase (in.)	51·5	42	49
Ground clear. (in.)	5·5	4	3·5
Seat height (in.)	29·5	26·5	28·5 to 36
Width (in.)	27	22·5	23
Length (in.)	80	64	63
Dry weight (lb)	270	120	98
Power: bhp	10	3·8	1·7
@ rpm	5600	9000	5500

1 from 1955 with 0·015 in. gaps. **2** 1955—0·010. **3** 1955—0·012.
4 1955—3·00 × 19. **5** 1955—WM2.

Model	Leader	Arrow	Super Sports	200 Arrow
Year from	**1958**	**1960**	**1961**	**1964**
Year to	**1965**	**1964**	**1965**	**1965**
Bore (mm)	54	54	54	48·5
Stroke (mm)	54	54	54	54
Capacity (cc)	247	247	247	199·5
Compression ratio (to 1)	8·25 **1**	8·25 **1**	10	9·5
Ignition timing degree	20	20	20	

Model	Leader	Arrow	Super Sports	200 Arrow
Year from	**1958**	**1960**	**1961**	**1964**
Year to	**1965**	**1964**	**1965**	**1965**
Points gap (in.)	0·015	0·015	0·015	
Tyre (in.)	3·25 × 16	3·25 × 16	3·25 × 16	3·25 × 16
Rim front	WM2	WM2		
Rim rear	WM2	WM2		
Brake front dia. (in.)	6	6	6	6
Brake front width (in.)	1·12	1·12	1·12	1·12
Brake rear dia. (in.)	6	6	6	6
Brake rear width (in.)	1·12	1·12	1·12	1·12
Front suspension	trailing link	trailing link	trailing link	trailing link
Rear type	s/a	s/a	s/a	s/a
Petrol tank (Imp. gal)	2·5 **2**	2·5 **2**	3·0	3·0
Box capacity (Imp. pint)	1·0	1·0	1·0	1·0
Chaincase (Imp. pint)	0·75	0·75	0·75	0·75
Ignition system	coil	coil	coil	coil
Generator type	alternator	alternator	alternator	alternator
Output (Watts)	50 **3**	50 **3**	50 **3**	55
Battery (Volt)	6	6	6	6
Wheelbase (in.)	51	51	51	51
Ground clear. (in.)	5	5	5	5
Seat height (in.)	30	28·5	28·5	28·5
Width (in.)	24·5	24	25·2	25·2
Length (in.)	73·5	77·5	78	78
Dry weight (lb)	300 **4**	275	278	278
Power: bhp	16 **5**	16 **5**	20	14
@ rpm	6400	6400	6600	6250

1 1961—10·0. **2** 1961—3·0. **3** 1962—55. **4** 330 with all options.
5 1961—17·5.

Transmission data

All models other than the Pixie used Burman gearboxes during the postwar era. These varied in type with CP and BA versions being fitted up to 1951 and GB types from 1952 to 1959. Wide ratios were fitted for trials use. The Colt was fitted with a lightweight box and that used in the twin two-strokes was special to them. The Pixie used the same gearbox as the BSA Beagle it was derived from.

Gearing changes were generally done by varying the engine and gearbox sprockets. Normally the big four strokes kept to 44 teeth clutch and 47 teeth rear wheel sprockets, only the FH varying due to its BSA origin. The Pixie had gear primary drive.

To avoid repetition of the same notes for many models the details of gearbox types, box ratios, sprockets and gearing is given for each model by year. The intermediate ratios may be calculated from this data.

Transmission on all models except Pixie was by chain and all 350 cc and above machines used $\frac{1}{2} \times \frac{5}{16}$ in. primary and $\frac{5}{8} \times \frac{3}{8}$ in. final drive chains. The Colt used the same primary and $\frac{1}{2} \times \frac{7}{32}$ final and the Leader series used $\frac{3}{8} \times \frac{7}{32}$ in. primary and $\frac{1}{2} \times \frac{5}{16}$ in. final drive. On the Pixie the final drive was $\frac{1}{2} \times \frac{3}{16}$ in. while on the Ariel 3 it was $\frac{3}{8} \times \frac{7}{32}$ in. with the pedalling chain $\frac{1}{2} \times \frac{1}{8}$ in.

Gearing

Model	Year	Sprockets E	C	G	W	Top ratio	Gearbox
4F/5	1931–32	21	44	19	47	5·183	BA1
4F/6	1932–36	21	44	19	47	5·183	BA1
	1939	24	44	16	47	5·385	CP2
	or	23	44	16	47	5·620	CP2
4G	1937–39	25	44	19	47	4·354	BA2
	1945–51	24	44	19	47	4·535	BA2
Mk I	1952–53	24	44	19	47	4·535	GB7
4G Mk 2	1953–55	26	44	19	47	4·186	GB7
	1956–59	25	44	19	47	4·354	GB7
KG, KH	1948	23	44	18	47	4·995	CP1
	1949–51	21	44	19	47	5·183	BA1
KH	1952–57	21	44	19	47	5·183	GB6
KHA	1952–53	21	44	19	47	5·183	GB6
FH	1954–56	24	42	19	47	4·329	GB33
	1957–59	24	44	19	47	4·535	GB33
W/NG	1940–44	20	44	18	47	5·744	CP1
NG	1945–50	18	44	20	47	5·744	CP1
NH	1945–51	18	44	20	47	5·744	CP1
	1952–59	19	44	19	47	5·728	GB5
VG	1945–50	19	44	23	47	4·732	BA1
VH	1945–51	19	44	23	47	4·732	BA1
	1952–59	23	44	19	47	4·732	GB6
VHA	1952–53	23	44	19	47	4·732	GB6
VB	1945–51	19	44	23	47	4·732	BA1
	1952–58	22	44	19	47	4·947	GB6
HT3	1957–59	17	44	18	47	6·758	GB wide
VCH (trials)	1949–51	19	44	18	47	6·047	BA wide
	1952–53	19	44	19	47	5·728	GB trials
VCH (M–X)	1949–51	19	44	19	47	5·728	BA
	1952–53	21	44	19	47	5·183	GB
HT/HT5	1954–59	18	44	19	47	6·047	GB wide
HS	1954–59	18	44	19	47	6·047	GB
LH	1954–59	17	43	17	47	6·993	GB30
Leader, Arrow	1958–65	22	50	18	47	5·934	Leader
200 Arrow	1964–65	22	50	18	49	6·187	Leader

Gearbox ratios

BA1, BA2, CP1, CP2, BA	1·0, 1·28, 1·76, 2·67
GB, GB5, GB6, GB7, GB33	1·0, 1·307, 1·7, 2·654
GB30	1·0, 1·21, 1·66, 2·5
BA wide	1·0, 1·51, 2·08, 3·16
GB wide	1·0, 1·57, 2·44, 3·2
GB trials	1·0, 1·48, 2·01, 3·13
Leader	1·0, 1·31, 1·86, 3·20

Pixie ratios

1963–65 Primary gearing 3·3:1
Overall gearing 11·2, 14·8, 23·1, 30·3
Gearbox ratios 1·0, 1·318, 2·059, 2·985.

Colours

1945

NG, **VG**, **VB**: black frame, forks, oil tank, toolbox, hubs, wheel rims. Petrol tank chrome plated with black side and top panels lined gold. Chrome plated headlamp rim, exhaust system.

NH, **VH**: as **NG** except tank panels in red and wheel rims chrome plated with red centres lined gold.

4G: as **NH** with option of black for tank panels and rim centres.

1946–47

All: no change.

1948

All: fork seal holder chrome plated.

KG: as **NG** except rims as **NH** in black.

KH: as **NH**.

1949

4G, **KG**, **KH**: chrome-plated front brake backplate.

Others: as 1948.

1950

All: as 1949.

KG, **NG**, **VB**: option with tank panels green and wheel rims chrome plated with green centres.

VCH: as **VH** except light alloy mudguards and polished front brake backplate.

1951

All: chrome plated battery clamp, finish as 1950, green option for **KG** and **VB** only.

Early 1951

All painted tanks, gold lined, with pressed brass badge with enamel filling.

NH, **VH**, **VCH**, **KH**: red.

VB, **KG**: red or black.

4G: red or black

1952

NH, **VH**, **KH**, **4G**: as late 1951.

VB: as late 1951, green tank option.

VCH: as 1950.

VHA: as **VH**.

1953

4G Mk 1, **4G Mk 2**, **KH**, **KHA**, **VH**, **VHA**: Wedgwood blue for all painted parts except headlamp shell in black, white lining to tank and mudguards, wheel rims chrome plated with blue centres, white lined. Option in deep claret with gold lining to same finish.

NH: deep claret tank and rim centres, remainder black. Option in all deep claret or all blue.

VB: all black including rims. Options of tank only in blue or green, also options of all blue or all deep claret.

VCH: deep claret frame, forks, oil tank, tank, rear stand, rim centres. Tank and rims lined gold, alloy mudguards.

1954

4G: black with gold lining; chrome plated tank flutes and band along base of each tank side extending partway to rear; round plastic tank badge in red and gold; chrome plated wheel rims with black centres, gold lined.

NH, **VH**, **KH**, **FH**: deep claret, gold lined; chrome plated tank flutes and deep band running back to kneegrip; tank badge as **4G** centred on top edge of band; wheel rims as **4G** in deep claret.

VB: black; chrome plated tank flutes, no side band, gold lined; small linear badges.

HS, **HT**: black frame, forks, oil tanks; chrome plated mudguards, light alloy option; tank red, gold lined, chrome plated kneegrip area, round badges, light alloy option.

LH: prototype in black, production model in deep Brunswick green including dualseat; chrome plated wheel rims and tank flutes.

1955

4G: as 1954 or in deep claret.

LH: no change.

FH, **KH**: as 1954 except chrome rims, no centre colour.

NH, **VH**, **HT**, **HS**: as 1954.

VB: s/a model as **NH** in claret, round badges; rigid model as 1954.

1956

4G: deep claret, gold lined; wheel rims chrome plated only; tank badges chrome yellow and black with chrome surround; polished alloy strip on cowl top.

FH, **KH**: generally as 1955 in deep claret; no chrome plated side bands on tank, twin horizontal lines, badges as **4G**, cowl strip as **4G**.

NH, **VH**, **VB**: badges as **4G**, rims plated only, cowl strip as **4G**.

LH: no change.

HT: tank and mudguards in light alloy.

HS: steel tank and mudguards, light alloy mudguard option.

1957

4G: as 1956 plus option in black.

NH, **VH**, **KH**, **FH**, **VB**: deep claret as 1956, no tank flutes, new white tank lining, chrome plated tank top band.

LH: two tone with deep Brunswick green for frame, forks, chaincase; light green tank, mudguards, oil tank, toolbox. Chrome plated battery strap, polished tank top strap.

HT, **HS**: as 1956.

1958
4G, **LH**, **NH**, **VH**, **VB**, **FH**: deep claret as 1957 with options in all black or glamour red and black frame and forks.
HT, **HS**: as 1956.
Leader: Admiralty grey forks, mudguards, main beam, front shield, side panels, all out of sight details, chaincase, footrests, brake pedal, legshields. Cherokee red or oriental blue for headlamp cowl, tank and main shell, tail section with seat to match. Fork spats grey with chrome flash, cast silencer ends with satin finish, chrome plated silencer bodies, rims, exhaust pipes.
1959
4G, **FH**, **VH**, **NH**, **LH**: as 1958.
HT, **HS**: as 1956.
Leader: as 1958.
1960
Leader: as 1958 plus option colour of seal grey added.
Arrow: dark seal grey—false tank, fork spats, gearbox cover, points cover, rear number plate housing, air filter housing, silencer ends, hubs. Black dualseat, remainder in Admiralty grey as **Leader**.
1961
Leader: as 1960.
Arrow: as 1960 with options in red or blue in place of seal grey.
Sports: polychromatic gold false tank, rear number plate mounting; polished primary chaincase; red pvc bar grips; whitewall tyres; chrome plated gearbox cover, points cover, toolbox lid, fork spats, lifting handles, air filter body; remainder as standard.
1962
All: base colour in ivory.
Leader: as 1958 in red, blue, seal grey or black with ivory; fork spats retained chrome flash.
Arrow: black tank, hubs, gearbox and points covers, silencer ends.
Sports: as 1961.
1963
Leader, **Sports**: as 1962.
Arrow: as 1962 plus option in red and ivory.
Pixie: main frame, forks, front mudguard in ivory; rear fork, chaincase, seat, handlebars in Cherokee red or oriental blue.
1964
All: as 1963.
200 Arrow: British racing green or aircraft (royal) blue for tank and chaincase, remainder in ivory including gearbox cover; **200 Arrow** tank badges.
1965
All: as 1964.
1970
Ariel 3: Bushfire orange, Everglade green, Pacific blue for main beam, forks, engine cowl and frame, wheel hub centres; white headlamp shell, front apron, front mudguard, legshields, sides of rear panelling.

Engine and frame numbers

Ariel used a series of letter prefixes for engines and frames with the number following. There would seem to be no sequence to these much of the time and although there may be a common letter for a year it may not be the same for engine, rigid frame and sprung frame. Even where this exists there may be an exception or two. The use of a suffix letter 'C' indicates a change of cam form. Serial numbers generally started at 101 each year but for certain models ran on and did this for all in 1959 and later. The Leader series ran from 101 up with prefix T and different suffixes for the various models and for the cylinder head change.

			Frame	
Year	**Model**	**Engine**	**rigid**	**spring**
1931	4F	R	R	
1932	4F/5	R	T or D	
	4F/6	T	T	
1933	4F/5	RA	Y	
	4F/6	TA	Y	
1934	4F/6	VA	Y	
1935	4F/6	WA	Y	
1936	4F/6	WB	F	
1937	4G	EC	CP	
1938	4G	DC or DD	P	
1939	4F	EE	P	AX
	4G & 4H	DE	P	AX
1940	4F	EH	P	AX
	4G & 4H	DH	P	AX
1941–44	W/NG	BH	XG	
1945–47	NG, NH	BK	AP	

Year	Model	Engine	Frame rigid	Frame spring
	VG, VH	CK	BP	
	VB	CK	BP	
	4G	DK	XP	
1948	NG, NH	AJ	BP	BX
	VG, VH	BJ	BP	BX
	KG, KH	PJ	VP	CX
	VB	BJ	BP	BX
	4G	CJ	XP	AX
1949	NG, NH	DJ	RF	SF
	VG, VH	EJ	RF	SF
	KG, KH	HT	HH or RH	HS
	VB	EJ	RF	SF
	4G	FJ	GR	GS
1950	NG, NH	KL	AB	AC
	VG, VH	MN	AB	AC
	VCH	MN	AB	
	KG, KH	OP	GD	LL
	VB	MN	AB	AC
	4G	JJ	TD	CW
1951	NH	RA	WA	SA
	VH	RB	WA	SA
	VCH	RB	WA	
	KG, KH	RC	WB	SB
	VB	RB	WA	SA
	4G	RD	WC	SC
9/51	KG (last)	RC 1452	WB 575	
1952	NH	TB	OA 199	SD
	VH	TC 226	OA 129	SD
	VCH	TR	OR 115	
	COMP	CO	COM	
	VHA	TCA	OA	SD 573
	KH	TE	OB	SE
	VB	TC	OA	SD 2972
	4G	TM	OC	SV
1953	NH	XA	AM	AS
	VH	XC	AM	AS
	VCH	XE	MA	
	VHA	XD	AM	AS
	KH	XF	BW	BS
	KHA	XFA	BW	BS
	VB	XB	AM	AS
	4G Mk 1	XH	EJ	ES
	4G Mk 2	XJ	EJ	ES
2/53	4G Mk 1 (last)	XH 1303	EJ 266	ES 266
9/53	VCH (last)	TR 219	OR 215	
	VHA (last)	XD 327		AS 2680
	KHA (last)	XFA 560	BW 287	
1954	LH	PA		KN
	NH	PB	KW	KS
	VH	PD	KW	KS
	HT	PT	KT	
	HS	PS		KSS
	KH	PH		KS
	VB	PE	KW	VS
	FH	PJ		KS
	4G	PL		KR
1955	LH	LA		LS
	NH	LB		DU
	VH	LC		DU
	HT	LJ	TF	
	HS	LK		DUS
	KH	LE		DU
	VB	LD	RF	DU
	FH	LF		DU
	4G	GL		PS
1956	LH	ALA 4139		MT
	NH	MA		PR
	VH	MB		PR
	HT	MJ		RT
	HS	MH		PRS
	KH	MD		PR
	VB	MC		PR
	FH	MLF		PR
	4G	ML		GM

Year	Model	Engine	Frame
1957	LH	BLA 5900	ST 1830
	NH	AMA 2200	APR 5200
	HT3	TH	RT 2221
	VH	AMB 920	APR 5200
	HT5	NJ 185	RT 195
	HS	NH 330	PRS 330
	KH	AMD 715	APR 5200
	VB	AMC 580	APR 5200
	FH	NLF 2858	APR 5200
	4G	NML 650	GM 650
8/57	KH (last)	AMD 1101	APR 8333
1958	LH	CBLA 7370	CST 3375
	NH	CAMA 4200	CAPR 9790
	HT3	TH	CRT
	VH	CAMB 1431	CAPR 9790
	HT5	CNJ 265	CRT 330
	HS	CNH 427	CPRS 449

Year	Model	Engine	Frame
	VB	CAMC 1065	CAPR 9790
	FH	CNLF 4230	CAPR 9790
	4G	CNML 1305	CGM 1310
1959	LH	CBLA 8435	CST 4032
	NH	CAMA 5174	CAPR 13618
	HT3	TH 140	CRT 561
	VH	CAMB 5174	CAPR 13618
	HT5	CNJ 379	CRT 569
	HS	CNH 475	CPRS 484
	FH	CNLF 5838	CAPR 13145
	4G	CNML 1836	CGM 1868
1/59	VB (last)	CAMC 1367	CAPR
8/59	LH (last)	CBLA 8577	CST 4022
	NH (last)	CAMA 5636	CAPR 13943
	HT3 (last)	TH 138	CRT 617
	VH (last)	CAMB 1911	CAPR 13751
	HT5 (last)	CNJ 413	CRT 627
	HS (last)	CNH 492	CPRS 514
	FH (last)	CNLF 6073	CAPR 12135

Lightweights

	Engine and Frame				
Year	Leader	Arrow	Sports	200	Pixie
7·58	T101A				
12·59		T9165S			
last A and S	T17200A	T17200S			
10·60	T17591B	T17441T	T20384G		
9·61	T26293B	T26293T	T26293G		
9·63	T32800B	T32800T	T32800G		
11·63					P101
1·64		T33995T			
4·64				T33701H	
9·64	T34700B		T34725G	T34650H	P1517
8·65	T35462B		T35452G	T35506H	
Suffix letters	A and B	S and T	G	H	

Carburettor settings

Model	Year	Amal type	Size	Main	Pilot	Slide	Needle pos.	Needle jet
LH 250 cc	1954	275	$\frac{13}{16}$	75		5/3	3	std
LH 250 cc	1955–58	375	$\frac{13}{16}$	90	25	$3\frac{1}{2}$	2	·105
W/NG 350 cc	1940–45	76	1	150		6/4	3	·107
W/NG 350 cc	1940–45	75	$\frac{7}{8}$	110		5/4	3	std
W/NG 350 cc	1940–45	275	$\frac{7}{8}$	120		5/4	3	std
NG 350 cc	1946–50	275	$\frac{7}{8}$	120		5/4	3	std
NH 350 cc	1946–54	276	1	150		6/4	3	·107
NH 350 cc	1955–58	376	1	200	25	$3\frac{1}{2}$	3	·106
HT3 350 cc	1957–58	376	1	200	25	$3\frac{1}{2}$	3	·106
VG 500 cc	1946–50	276	$1\frac{1}{16}$	170		6/4	3	std
VH 500 cc	1946–54	289	$1\frac{1}{8}$	200		29/3	3	std
VH 500 cc	1955–59	376	$1\frac{1}{16}$	200	30	$3\frac{1}{2}$	3	·106
HS 500 cc	1954	TT9	$1\frac{3}{16}$	380		6	4	·109
500 scrambler	1955–56	TT9	$1\frac{3}{16}$	400		6	3	·109
HS 500 cc	1956–58	389	$1\frac{3}{16}$	380	30	$3\frac{1}{2}$	3	·106
HT5 500 cc	1956–58	376	$1\frac{1}{16}$	200	30	3	3	·106
KG 500 cc	1946–52	276	$\frac{15}{16}$	140		6/3	3	·107
KH 500 cc	1946–54	276	1	150		6/3	3	·107
KHA 500 cc	1952–53	276	1	150		6/3	3	·107
KH 500 cc	1955–58	376	1	200	30	$3\frac{1}{2}$	3	·106
VA 500 cc	1940–45	276	1	140		6/4	3	·107
VB 600 cc	1946–54	276	1	160		6/4	3	std

Model	Year	Amal type	Size	Main	Pilot	Slide	Needle pos.	Needle jet
VB 600 cc	1955–58	376	1	220	30	5	2	·106
Four 500/600 cc	1931–36	74	$\frac{21}{32}$	90		4/4	3	·106
FH 650 cc	1954	276	$1\frac{1}{16}$	170		6/4	2	std
FH 650 cc	1955–59	376	$1\frac{1}{16}$	240	25	$3\frac{1}{2}$	3	·106
Leader and Arrow								
250 cc	1958–65	375	$\frac{7}{8}$	170	30	$3\frac{1}{2}$	3	·105
Super Sports Arrow	1962–65	376	$1\frac{1}{16}$	230	30	$3\frac{1}{2}$	3	·105
200 Arrow	1964–65	375	$\frac{13}{16}$	120	30	$3\frac{1}{2}$	3	·104
Pixie	1964	19	$\frac{1}{2}$	55	15	3	3	·104
Pixie	1964–65	19	$\frac{1}{2}$	50	15	3	3	·106

Square 4

From 1937 this model fitted a Solex instrument and from 1954 an SU. Settings are as below

Solex	600 cc 1939	1000 cc 1937–38	1000 cc 1938–52	1000 cc 1953
Type	26FHDT	26FHDT	26AHD	26AHD
Choke tube	20	23	23	23
Main jet	100 × 58	115 × 58	120	120
Air correction jet			150	170
Pilot jet	055	055	070	060
GA jet			3	3
GS jet			100	100
Well	50443/L1	50443/L1		5·1
Jet cap	19 × 140 × 2	19 × 140 × 2	51861/L2	51861/L2
Needle valve	2	2	2	2

SU – 1954 to 1959

SU type MC2 fitted to engines commencing number PL.101.1954.

Needle type	GN
Jet size	0·090 in.

Prices

The UK prices of the machines of the postwar period are set out in the tables below. Included in them is the purchase tax payable then except in the 1945 figures which are basic.

During the early 1950s many of the alterations were due to tax rate changes and the basic figure moved little in those days.

Date	NG	NH	VH	VG	VCH	VHA
20.9.45	£95.+	£101.+	£112.+	£104.+		
27.6.46	£125.14s. 7d.	£138. 8s. 7d.	£156. 4s. 3d.	£139.14s. 0d.		
29.8.46	£132. 1s. 7d.	£138. 8s. 7d.	£156. 4s. 3d.	£144.15s. 7d.		
10.4.47	£142. 4s. 9d.	£149.17s. 3d.	£168.18s. 2d.	£156. 4s. 3d.		
13.10.49	£147. 6s. 5d.	£154.18s.11d.	£173.19s.10d.	£161. 5s.11d.	£228.12s. 0d.	
1.2.51		£161. 5s.10d.	£173.19s.10d.		£228.12s. 0d.	
1.10.51		£172.10s. 0d.	£194. 4s. 5d.		£217. 4s. 6d.	£207. 0s. 0d.
6.11.52		£172.10s. 0d.	£194. 4s. 5d.		£207. 0s. 0d.	£207. 0s. 0d.
23.4.53		£163. 2s. 6d.	£183.13s. 4d.		£195.15s. 0d.	£195.15s. 0d.
15.10.53	**LH**	£180. 0s. 0d.	£198. 0s. 0d.			
6.11.53	£132. 0s. 0d.					
9.9.54	£134. 8s. 0d.	£186. 0s. 0d.	£198. 0s. 0d.		**HT**	**HS**
18.11.54					£192. 0s. 0d.	£222. 0s. 0d.
14.3.55	£140. 8s. 0d.	£195. 0s. 0d.	£205.16s. 0d.			
8.9.55	£140. 8s. 0d.	£200. 8s. 0d.	£208.16s. 0d.			
26.4.56	£145. 1s. 7d.	£207. 1s. 7d.	£215.15s. 3d.		£220. 2s. 0d.	£248. 0s. 0d.
				HT3	**HT5**	
8.11.56				£220. 2s. 0d.	£220 2s. 0d.	
26.9.57	£155.18s. 9d.	£230.15s. 9d.	£237. 0s. 6d.	£243 5s. 3d.	£243. 5s. 3d.	£268. 4s. 3d.
23.4.59	£150.15s. 8d.	£223. 3s. 2d.	£229. 3s. 9d.			

	VB	KG	KH	FH	4G	4G Mk2
20.9.45	£100.+				£155.+	
27.6.46	£135.17s.10d.				£213. 7s. 3d.	
29.8.46	£139.14s. 0d.				£213. 7s. 3d.	
10.4.47	£152. 8s. 0d.				£228.12s. 0d.	
27.11.47		£185. 8s. 5d.	£196.17s. 0d.			
13.10.49	£157. 9s. 8d.	£190.10s. 1d.	£201.18s. 8d.		£246. 7s. 8d.	
1.2.51	£165. 2s. 0d.	£190.10s. 1d.	£201.18s. 8d.		£260. 7s. 0d.	
1.10.51	£181. 8s.11d.		£222. 6s. 8d.		£281. 2s. 3d.	
		KHA				
6.11.52	£181. 8s.11d.	£235. 2s. 3d.	£222. 6s. 8d.		£281. 2s. 3d.	£287.10s. 0d.
23.4.53	£171.11s. 8d.	£222. 6s. 8d.	£210. 5s. 0d.		£265.16s. 8d.	£271.17s. 6d.
15.10.53	£170. 8s. 0d.		£216. 0s. 0d.	£230. 8s. 0d.		£294. 0s. 0d.
		VB(S)				
9.9.54	£174. 0s. 0d.	£186. 0s. 0d.	£222. 0s. 0d.	£230. 8s. 0d.		£294. 0s. 0d.
14.3.55	£180.12s. 0d.	£193.16s. 0d.	£230. 8s. 0d.	£242. 8s. 0d.		£308. 8s. 0d.
8.9.55		£198. 0s. 0d.	£234. 0s. 0d.	£244.16s. 0d.		£312. 0s. 0d.
26.4.56		£204.12s. 0d.	£241.16s. 0d.	£252.19s. 3d.		£322. 8s. 0d.
26.9.57		£222. 1s. 1d.		£266.19s. 4d.		£336.16s. 6d.
23.4.59				£258. 2s. 9d.		£325.13s. 9d.

	Leader	Arrow	Sports	200 Arrow	Pixie
17.7.58	£209.11s. 7d.				
23.4.59	£202.13s. 0d.				
10.12.59	£197.16s. 6d.	£167.13s. 5d.			
6.10.60	£199.18s. 9d.	£171.17s.10d.			
19.1.61			£187.11s. 5d.		
10.8.61	£203. 7s. 1d.	£174.16s. 7d.	£190.15s. 7d.		
7.9.61	£203. 7s. 1d.	£179. 2s. 6d.	£190.15s. 7d.		
22.3.62	£213. 9s. 6d.	£188. 0s. 5d.	£200. 5s. 9d.		
18.4.62	£209.17s. 9d.	£184.17s. 2d.	£196.18s. 5d.		
6.9.62	£219.12s. 0d.	£192. 0s. 0d.	£206. 8s. 0d.		£79.10s. 0d.
6.11.63					£81.18s. 0d.
11.3.64			£211.14s. 1d.		
7.5.64	£225. 0s. 0d.	£196.15s. 6d.	£211.14s. 1d.	£187.10s. 4d.	
6.5.65					£85. 1s. 0d.

Ariel 3 in July 1970 £110. 0s. 0d.

Accessories

For the traditional 4 stroke machines the following were on offer and over the years the prices varied but little.

Frame with link rear suspension	£19. 1s. 0d.
Speedometer	£5. 1s. 8d.
q.d. rear wheel	£3.16s. 3d.
Pillion seat	£1.11s. 9d.
Pillion rests	15s.11d.
Rear carrier	£1. 2s. 3d.
Mag-dyno lighting set for VCH	£11.10s. 0d.
Rear chaincase (not for 4G or LH)	£3. 2s. 0d.

Leader

Parking light	19s. 0d.
Inspection lamp	15s. 1d.
Carrier and straps	£1.19s.10d.
Prop stand	£1. 8s. 0d.
Front stand	12s. 8d.
Pannier cases	£9. 7s. 0d.
Pannier bags	£2.10s. 0d.
Neutral indicator	£1. 4s. 2d.
8 day clock	£5. 8s. 7d.
Flashers (on panniers)	£7. 9s. 7d.
Flashers (no panniers)	£7.19s. 3d.
Trip speedo (extra)	9s. 8d.
Dualseat cover	9s. 4d.
Mirror pair	£1. 6s. 3d.
Windscreen extension	£1. 5s. 0d.
Rear fender and reflector	£1.17s.10d.
Supplementary rear springs	10s. 0d.

Arrow

Front stand	12s. 8d.
Prop stand	£1.12s. 7d.
Carrier	£1.11s. 1d.
Seat cover	9s. 4d.
Dualseat grab handle	6s. 3d.
Whitewall tyres	£1.11s. 0d.
Motoplas screen	
2 level petrol tap	4s. 0d.

Pixie

Speedometer	£3. 3s. 0d.
Legshields	£4. 4s. 0d.
Rear carrier	£1.15s. 0d.
Pair mirrors	£1. 5s. 0d.
Bag hook	8s. 0d.
Screen	£4.10s. 0d.
Panniers	£6. 6s. 0d.
Rear fender	£1.16s. 0d.
Shopping basket	£1. 5s. 0d.

Ariel 3

Carrier basket	£1.15s. 0d.
Screen	£2.12s. 6d.

Model recognition

These notes are to some extent a precis of the main text and should be used in conjunction with it and the other appendices.

Fours, twins and singles

1945

All: girder forks, rigid frame, saddle, instrument panel, generally as 1939 models.
4G: valanced mudguards, tubular silencer, '1000' on timing case.
NG: small oil and petrol tanks, more ground clearance.
NH: tanks as NG.
VG: valanced mudguards.
All ohv singles: 2 port head option, high level pipe option for single or two port heads.
VB: valanced mudguards, Brooklands silencer and fishtail.

June 1946

4G, NH, VH: telescopic forks and front brake with fulcrum adjuster.

1947

NG, VG: forks and front hub as **4G**.
All: spring frame option.

1948

All: chronometric speedometer.
KG, KH: twins introduced with telescopics, saddle, rigid frame or spring frame as option.

1949

All: forks modified, neater rear number plate, finned exhaust pipe clips, dynamo output increased.
4G: alloy engine, coil ignition, two rocker boxes, integral exhaust manifolds and inlet tract, two lobe shock absorber, 'Square Four' on timing case.
KG, KH: gearing lowered.
All singles: prop stand, air filter option.
NG, NH: 2 port head and high level pipe options continued.
VG, VH: no options for head or pipe.

1950

All: saddle height raised, tubular mudguard stays, prefocus headlight, rear brake pedal modified.
4G: speedometer mounted in fork bridge, new tank panel layout, qd rear wheel, new prop stand, polished crankcase and block base and fin edges.
KG, KH: speedometer as **4G**, solid tappets, new tank, options of qd rear, ribbed front tyre, air cleaner.
Singles: light switch in headlamp shell, options as twins.
VCH: introduced in rigid frame only.
Later in year **NG** and **VG** discontinued.

1951

All: die-cast alloy top crown carrying speedometer, ammeter and light switch in panel in headlamp shell, no tank instrument panel, tank capacity increased, central filler cap, rear mudguard stay modified, lifting handle, non-detachable rear mudguard tail, guard pivots from beneath seat, two piece battery clamp, front number plate surround, barrel saddle springs.
4G: oil gauge in petrol tank behind filler cap, 8 in. rear brake, die-cast backplate, ignition switch under seat, 20 ah battery.
KG, KH: oil gauge as **4G**, more fins on head and barrel, pipe run change, flywheel weight increased by 20 per cent, more rigid rocker box covers without slots. During year Millenite soft iron gears adopted behind cam sprockets for magneto and dynamo drive, no slipping clutch, normal screw and locknut for valve rockers. Late in year **KG** discontinued.
Singles: no oil gauge, single cam, forked exhaust cam follower, quietening ramps.

1952

All: prop stand moved forward, Burman GB gearbox adopted.
4G: tank capacity increased.
KH: new oil tank, revised cam form, revised big end oil hole.
All ohv singles: split skirt pistons, head gasket, more fin depth, new 6 pint oil tank (not **NH**).
VB: new barrel, more fin depth, alloy head, 9 studs, tubular silencer.
VCH: mudguard section change, frame fork end modified to increase ground clearance.
VHA: new model, all alloy engine, 5 stud Hunter crankcase.

1953

All road: cable rear brake with link suspension, underslung pilot lamp.
4G: Mk 1 continued until late in year.
4G, Mk 2: introduced with 4 pipe head, separate exhaust

manifolds and inlet tract, gear type oil pump, deeper block fins, Neoprene clutch inserts, raised gearing, 5 gallon tank, Diacon stop and tail lamp, sports front mudguard.
KH: new prop stand, Diacon stop and tail lamp.
KHA: new model, all alloy engine, separate rocker box lids, optional dualseat.
VH, VHA: new prop stand, dualseat option, Diacon rear lamp, rocker oil feed from return pipe.
NH: 6 pint oil tank, new prop stand, dualseat option, rocker oil feed from return pipe.
VCH: rocker oil feed as **NH**, dynamo and lights option. Late in year **KHA**, **VHA** and **VCH** discontinued.

1954
4G: Mk 2 only with link rear suspension as standard, SU carburettor, inlet tract extended across head, modified frame, tank flutes.
KH: iron barrel, alloy head with fixing as **KHA**.
FH: 650 cc A10 engine with Ariel outer timing case and rocker box.
KH, FH: s/a frame, dualseat, tank flutes, rod rear brake operation, later cable.
NH: s/a frame, dualseat, 4 gallon tank with flutes, new toolbox, oil tank and air filter.
VH: as **NH** plus alloy cylinder head on iron barrel with integral pushrod tunnels.
VB: rigid, link suspension option, saddle, 4 gallon tank with flutes.
HS: all alloy engine, s/a frame, dualseat, open pipe.
HT: all alloy engine, rigid frame, saddle.

1955
4G: steering lock in bottom fork crown, integral horn button, flexible fuel pipes.
Road twins and singles: lock and horn button as **4G**, longer rear brake pedal, extended rear mudguard, oil tank cap on front top corner of tank, chrome plated top piston ring, Monobloc, 19 in. front tyre.
KH, FH: flexible fuel pipes.
KH: inspection holes in rocker box sides with blanking plug, mid-year a chain tension blade replaced the Weller.
NH: flexible oil pipes, inspection holes in rocker box, plugs with lock for box caps.
VH: as **NH** plus smaller exhaust valve.
HS: as **NH** plus chrome top ring.
HT: as **HS** plus Monobloc.
VB: flexible oil pipes, s/a frame or rigid.

1956
All road: headlamp cowl, pilot bulb in reflector, speedometer plus light switch and ammeter in panel, combined dip switch and horn button, alloy handlebar clamp, during year separate flutes except **4G**.
4G: full width front hub, 8 pint oil tank, toolbox on left, straight pull throttle, gearing lowered. During year duplex timing chain, adjustable tensioner, revised dynamo speed, breather pipe extended inside timing case.
Road twins and singles: light alloy full width front and rear hubs, rear chain lubrication modification, rear chaincase option, rod and cable rear brake.
Road singles: straight pull throttle.
KH: called Fieldmaster, rocker oil feed modified.
FH: recommended sidecar gearing lowered.
NH: light alloy head, iron barrel with integral pushrod tunnels.
VB: available in s/a frame only.
HS: oil tank on left, air filter on right, Monobloc.
HT: s/a frame, short wheelbase, diamond pattern, 2 gallon tank.

1957
All road: deeper valance front mudguard with number plates on side, no forward stay, cross strap below headlamp, Ferodo segments in clutch drum.
Road twins and singles: $4\frac{1}{2}$ gallon single bolt tank with top strap and small kneegrips, no tank flutes, prop stand with pedal.
FH: gearing lowered, clutch sprocket plus two teeth.
KH: discontinued late in year.
HT5: smaller section front tyre.
HT3: new model, all alloy 350 cc version of **HT5**.

1958
No changes.
VB: discontinued late in year.

1959
No changes.
HS, HT5, HT3: discontinued early in year.
4G, FH, NH, VH: discontinued late in year.

Lightweights

Colt
1954: LH introduced, single cylinder, 4 speeds, plunger, damped teles, dualseat, separate rear mudguard stays. Pro-

totype had 3·00 in. tyres, Bantam silencer and 80 mph speedometer.
1955: Monobloc, ramp cam, clutch adjuster changed, 3·00 in. tyres, fatter pushrods, deeper and wider mudguards, rear stays in one piece.
1956: Transverse inlet tract with air filter on right, separate ignition and lighting switches.
1957: Ammeter between switches, new rear lamp, polished timing case, head and rocker box, no flutes.
1958: No changes.
1959: No changes, discontinued late in year.

Leader and Arrow

1958: Leader introduced.
1959: No changes.
1960: Leader: new filler cap.
Arrow: new model, cast iron hubs, fulcrum adjuster on rear brake only.
1961: Both: central plugs, oval rods, cast iron hubs with three ribs, remote front brake anchorage, 3 gallon tank, common swirl silencer, groove in contact breaker cover.
Leader: trip speedometer, turn indicators for models without panniers, plastic holder for inspection lamp.
Super Sports Arrow: new model, bigger carburettor, drop bars, ball end levers, flyscreen, folding kickstarter, two level petrol tap, prop stand fitted as standard.
1962: All: RM18 alternator, plug and socket connections to switches, key ignition switch, water flange on brake backplates, anti-squeal springs in brake shoes.
Arrows: louder horn.
1963: No change.
1964: No changes.
200 Arrow: new model, smaller bore and carburettor, 2 more teeth on rear wheel sprocket. Late in year standard **Arrow** discontinued.
1965: No changes. Late in year all models discontinued.

Pixie

1962: New model introduced late in year.
1963: Into production late in year.
1964: No changes.
1965: No changes, discontinued late in year.

Model charts

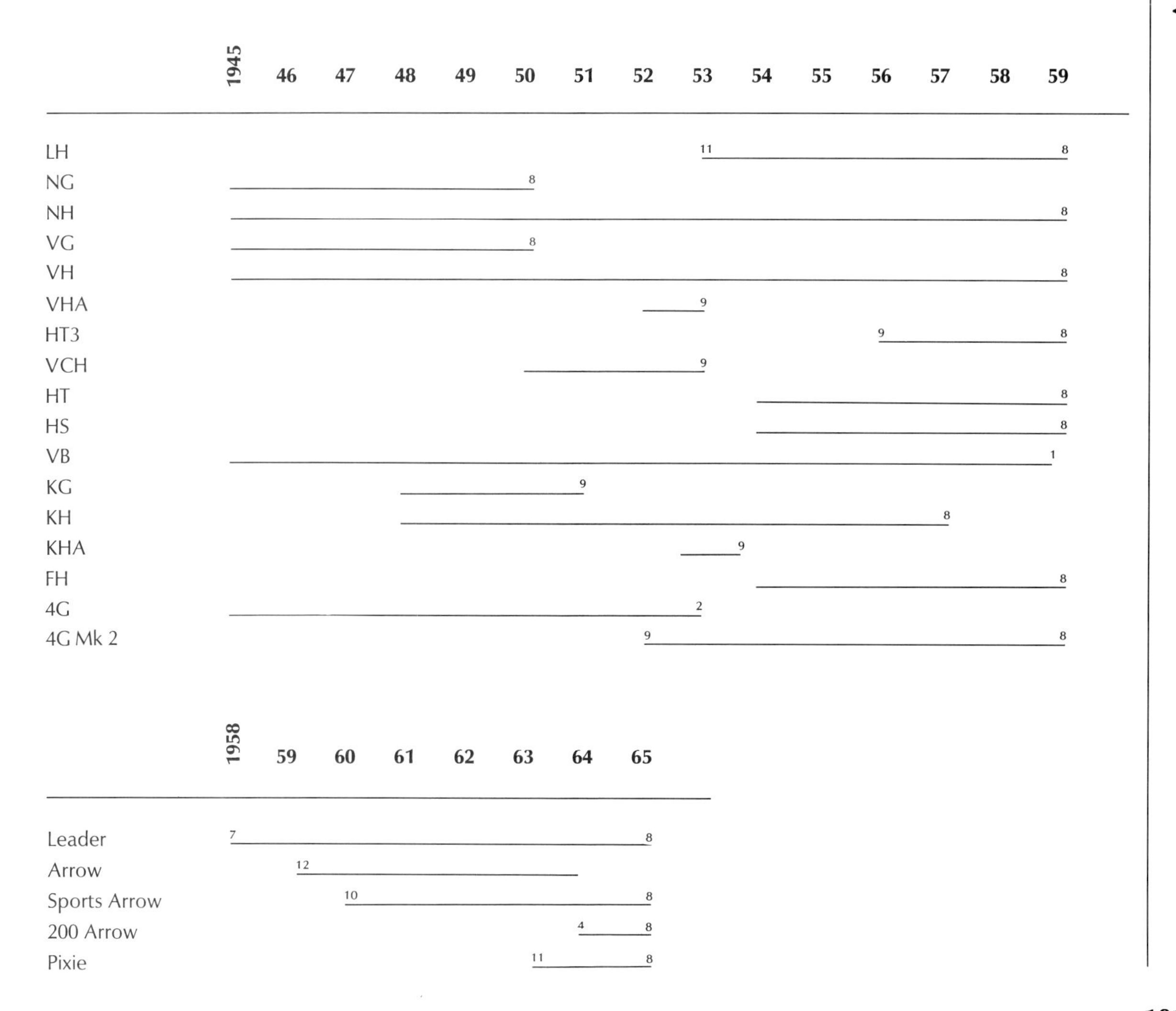

The Honda Stream of 1982 which like the Ariel 3 had three wheels and a hinge in the middle but no torsion bars to hold it up. They can afford a mistake